HORTON DAVIES, professor of religion at Princeton University since 1956, is a native of Cwmavon, Glamorganshire, Wales. A minister of the Congregational Church, Dr. Davies' hardest and most rewarding job in this capacity was as minister of Wallington Congregational Church in "Flying-Bomb Alley," South London, during the second World War.

Dr. Davies holds the M.A. and B.D. degrees from the University of Edinburgh, and the Ph.D. degree from Oxford. He was founder of the department of divinity, first professor of divinity, and dean of the faculty of divinity of Rhodes University, Grahamstown, South Africa, and later taught at Mansfield and Regent's Park colleges at Oxford.

The author of many books, Dr. Davies is also a frequent contributor to scholarly religious journals.

CHRISTIAN
WORSHIP

Its history and meaning

CHRISTIAN
WORSHIP

Its history and meaning

HORTON DAVIES

&

ABINGDON PRESS
New York   *Nashville*

CHRISTIAN WORSHIP—ITS HISTORY AND MEANING

Copyright © MCMLVII by Abingdon Press

Library of Congress Catalog Card Number: 57-9784

SET UP, PRINTED, AND BOUND BY THE
PARTHENON PRESS, AT NASHVILLE,
TENNESSEE, UNITED STATES OF AMERICA

DEDICATION

For three recent American immigrants

CHRISTINE
HUGH
PHILIP

pets and aversions

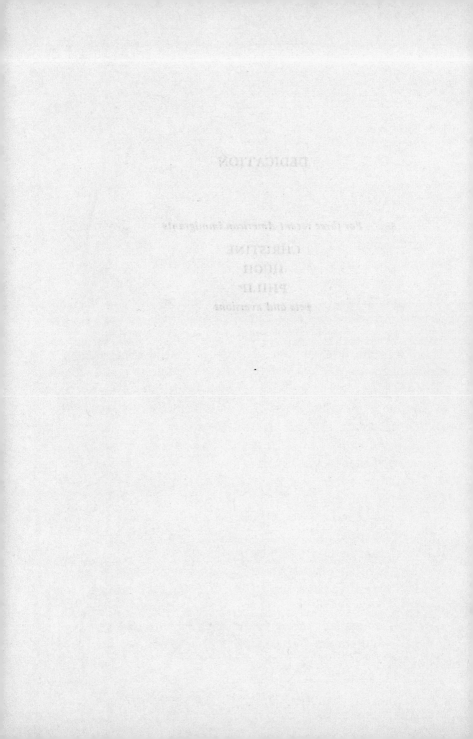

DEDICATION

for three recent American immigrants

CHRISTINE

HUGH

PHILIP

pets and creations

PREFACE

Christians of all denominations believe that God deserves and demands the tribute of their best thought, their deepest adoration, and their involvement in the social community. Theoretically these demands are met in the study, respectively, of theology, liturgiology, and social ethics. This book attempts to be a popular and at the same time accurate introduction to the second discipline—liturgiology—which is less pretentiously known as the history of the art of common worship. The author's concern is that more and more Christians shall share meaningfully in the corporate response to the love of God in Christ which is worship and which will irradiate their thinking and deepen their obligation to serve the community.

This book is therefore sent out with three subordinate purposes in mind:

First, to introduce the reader to the rich variety of forms of Christian worship still used in many parts of the world, so that he may look sympathetically at all types of worship, familiar or unfamiliar. Nowadays this is an ecumenical necessity, apart from being a delight of exploration.

Second, to explain to the reader the structure, the various parts and contents of the forms of common worship, so that he may co-operate in divine worship "with the heart and with the understanding."

Third, to show how relevant worship is to our day-to-day living in times of distraction, confusion, and stress through the criticism and comfort of the gospel to which our worship is the glad response.

HORTON DAVIES

CONTENTS

III. WORSHIP AND LIFE

I

THE HISTORY OF WORSHIP

CHAPTER 1

The Legacy of Temple and Synagogue

THE ORIGINS OF CHRISTIAN WORSHIP LIE IN THE TEMPLE AND in the synagogue, for Jesus and his disciples attended both, as faithful sons of Abraham. When "the followers of the Way" came to construct their own distinctively Christian type of worship, they had these examples to fall back upon. It is not surprising to find, therefore, that the worship of the early Christians is basically a modification of synagogue worship, with the special addition of the Lord's Supper. For this reason it is important to understand the character of synagogue worship, itself a simplification of the worship of the temple.

While the Jews remained in Palestine they worshiped in the temple, a splendid edifice, in which rested the ark of the covenant, the sacred symbol of God's peculiar care for his chosen people. God was believed to dwell in the Holy of holies. Its importance can be gathered from the description given by Evelyn Underhill:

It was . . . the "House" where God . . . was believed to dwell undiscerned; in a way so entirely supernatural, so completely transcending all our apprehensions and thoughts, that only the dark emptiness of this secret shrine could suggest it. For it is a mark of Israel's spiritual genius, that from the first the Jew

11

placed Reality within mystery: and here, perhaps, is the source of his intense aversion from all images of the Divine.[1]

The temple fulfilled three functions in the religious life of the Jews. It was an abiding reminder of the centrality of Yahweh (Jehovah) and his law in the national life. It also gave opportunity for the regular worship of him in praise and prayer and sacrifice. Third, it was the meeting place of the national religious assemblies that gathered to honor God at the festivals of the Jewish year.

The most important feature of the worship was the offering up of sacrifices. The teaching of Jeremiah and Ezekiel, and the humiliating experience of the Exile, helped to deepen the sense of sin among the Jews. This found expression in an extension of the sacrificial system. In particular, the "sin offering" was definitely made with the idea of atoning by a costly offering for sinning against God. The "trespass offering" was made as a confession of guilt and on the understanding that the man who had been wronged by a trespass would be requited by the worshiper. The deepest element of temple worship, its sacrificial emphasis, was to find its culmination in the sacrifice of the Cross. In that sense, the temple contributed to the understanding of the meaning of the Lord's Supper.

When thousands of the Jews were deported from Jerusalem into Babylon, and the temple was destroyed, they were forced to devise a new means of worshiping God. They were encouraged, in this resolve, by the teaching of the prophets that the nonsacrificial observances of the law were equally important. They then began to see that obedience to the commandments was itself a way of worshiping God. Furthermore, the later dispersion of the

---

[1] *Worship* (New York: Harper & Brothers, 1937), p. 205.

12

Jews to all parts of Asia Minor, North Africa, and Eastern Europe, necessitated the provision of meeting places for worship. As a result of these influences the synagogues emerged.

These were meant to provide a substitute for the temple worship. In their furnishings, for example, they were deliberately imitative of the temple. They had a movable chest, or "ark," in which the sacred scrolls of the Law and the prophetical writings were kept. There was also a ceremonial lampstand, recalling that used in the temple, and a veil or screen in front of the ark, as a substitute for the Holy of holies in the temple. Furthermore, parts of the liturgy of the temple were taken over, as, for instance, the recital of the Ten Commandments. The great difference was, however, that there was no place in the synagogue worship for the sacrifices which had been central in the temple worship. In their stead the earnest study of the Scriptures was substituted, in order that the worshipers might discover the will of God for common life. Also, the same purpose was served by attaching a school to each of the synagogues, in which the local Jewish boys were taught to read and to copy out the scriptures. Another feature of synagogue ritual was the absence of the priesthood, the position of the latter being taken by the ruler of the synagogue. He was usually the presiding elder, chosen for his nobility of character and for the esteem in which he was held by the local Jewish community.

The worship of the synagogue thus originated as a second-best alternative to temple worship, during the period of the Exile. Later, when the second and third temples were built, the synagogues were not abolished. All Jews in Palestine tried to observe the three major festivals in Jerusalem, but the synagogues were their regular meeting places for worship. In the case of the Jews of the Dispersion, the synagogues provided their only religious services. In the course of time the synagogues spread to every town and village in Palestine. Jesus owed his knowledge of the Scriptures to the instruction given at the village synagogue, and he continued to be a worshiper there during the years of his ministry (Luke 4:16).

The organization of the synagogue was simple. The communal affairs were in the hands of elders, from among whom the ruler of the synagogue was probaly selected. He controlled all its activities, superintending the services, the teaching in the school, and the distribution of alms to the poor. It was his duty to decide who should read the lessons and who should preach (Acts 13:15). He held his office for life. Next to the ruler, the minister held the most important office. He executed the orders of the ruler. He invited the appointed readers; he took out the scrolls from the "ark," and replaced them after the lessons had been read. When punishment was meted out, as a disciplinary measure in the synagogue, he wielded the scourge. He was a teacher in the synagogue school, and also assisted in the distribution of food to the poor.

The building was not an ornate edifice, like the temple. Such simple decoration as graced the exterior depended on the financial resources of the community, or on the generosity of private donors, a number of whom built and furnished synagogues at their own expense. Luke 7:5 provides one instance of this. The lintels were often decorated with simple religious motifs, such as a seven-branched candlestick, an open flower between two paschal lambs, vine leaves, or bunches of grapes. The furniture consisted simply of a raised platform, a movable chest or "ark," containing the scrolls of the Law and the Prophets, which were taken out of the ark on fast days and carried in procession.

By the end of the first century A.D. the form of service in the synagogue was no longer fluid, and it can be reconstructed with a fair degree of accuracy. The following account of first-century worship in a typical synagogue is based upon Paul Levertoff's reconstruction.[2]

The ruler would summon the minister to invite some member of the congregation to recite the *Shema* and Benedictions. This person, turning toward the congregation, would then begin: "Bless ye the Lord, the blessed One." The congregation would then respond: "Blessed be the Lord, the blessed One, for ever and ever." The leader would then recite the famous prayers, the *Yotzer* (meaning "who forms," so called from its designation of God as creator) and the *Ahabah* (meaning "Love," so called because it begins by emphasizing this attribute of God). The earliest form of the *Yotzer* was probably the following:

Blessed art thou, O Lord our God, King of the world, Former of light and Creator of darkness, Maker of peace and Creator of all things; who gives light in mercy to the earth and to those who live thereon, and in his goodness renews every day, continually, the work of creation. Let a new light shine over Zion and thy Messiah's light over us.

The *Ahabah,* one of the loveliest prayers in the Jewish liturgy, was said as follows:

With everlasting love hast thou loved us, O Lord our God; with great and exceeding compassion hast thou pitied us. Our Father, our King, for the sake of our fathers who trusted in

[2] "Synagogue Worship in the First Century," in *Liturgy and Worship,* eds. W. K. Lowther Clarke and Charles Harris (New York: The Macmillan Co., 1932; 1954).

thee, and to whom thou didst teach the statutes of life, be gracious also unto us, and teach us. Merciful Father, have mercy upon us; enlighten our eyes in the Law and let our hearts cleave unto thy commandments. Give us a single heart to love and fear thy Name. For in thy holy Name we trust; we rejoice and exult in thy salvation. Thou art a God who worketh salvation, and hast chosen us from all peoples and tongues, and hast brought us nigh unto thy great Name for ever in truth; to give thanks unto thee and to proclaim thy unity in love. Blessed art thou, O Lord, who hast chosen thy people Israel in love.

The *Yotzer* and *Ahabah* concluded, the *Shema* followed. This creed would be recited antiphonally. The leader would begin, "Hear, O Israel," and the congregation would respond by repeating that and then continuing to the end. As soon as the congregation reached the word "One," emphasizing the unity of God, the leader would respond with the words, "Blessed be the Name of the glory of his Kingdom for ever and ever."

The *Shema* derives its name from the first word *shema,* meaning "hear," and it is a recitation of the Jewish creed. It contains three paragraphs: Deut. 6:4-9; 11:13-21; and Num. 15:37-41. This was followed by the prayer *Emeth we-Yatzib* ("True and constant"), which is sometimes called the *Geullah* ("Redemption"). Originally this prayer was probably said in unison, and ran as follows:

True and constant, established and enduring, right and faithful, beloved and precious, desirable and lovely, awful and mighty, well-ordered and worthy of all acceptation, good and beautiful, is this word [reference to the preceding *Shema*] to us for ever. True it is that the God of eternity is our King, the Rock of Jacob—the shield of our salvation. From generation to generation he endureth, and his Name endureth, and his throne is established, and his Kingdom and Faith endure for ever. His words live and endure, they are faithful and desirable for ever and for all eternity, for our fathers and for us, for our children and for our generations, and for all the generations of the seed of Israel, thy servant. For the past and present generations it is a good and constant word for ever and ever; it is true and faithful, an established thing that shall never pass away. True it is that thou art indeed the Lord our God and the God of our fathers, our King, the King of our fathers, our Redeemer, the Redeemer of our fathers, our Creator, the Rock of our salvation, our Redeemer and Saviour from everlasting; such is thy Name; there is no God beside thee.

Then the ruler would bid the minister call upon an appropriate person to lead in reciting the "Eighteen Benedictions" (reduced to seven on a Sabbath). These prayers are partly expressions of praise to God, partly petitions for knowledge and for repentance and for material blessings, and partly intercessions for exiles, for judges and counselors and the chosen people. The Eighteenth Benediction is cited here because in all probability it dates from the time of Christ and is typical of this form of prayer:

Grant peace upon Israel thy people and upon thy city, and upon thine inheritance, and bless us all together. Blessed art thou, O Lord, the Maker of peace.

The benedictions would be recited by the person appointed, standing in front of the ark, and facing it.

The congregation would also stand and after each benediction would respond with "Amen." If any priests happened to be present at the service they would mount the platform between the sixth and seventh benedictions and pronounce the Aaronic blessing (Num. 6:24-26) with uplifted hands.

17

The prayers over, the lections from the Law and the Prophets would ensue. The lesson from the Pentateuch would probably be divided into seven parts, and as many readers from the congregation would be chosen. However, on Mondays and Thursdays, which were market days, only three lections were read by the same number of persons. The prophetic lesson then followed. With this the service would end. Both lessons were translated from the Hebrew into the vernacular, in most cases Aramaic.

If there happened to be present a suitable person, the ruler of the synagogue would bid the minister invite him to preach a sermon, much as is recorded in Acts 13:15: "If ye have any word of exhortation for the people, say on."

While there is no recorded instance of singing in the synagogue, it is very probable that those parts of the liturgy which were associated with the temple worship, such as the recitation of the Psalms and the Aaronic blessing, were sung.

CHAPTER 2

The Worship of the Apostolic Church

THE FIRST COMPANY OF CHRISTIANS WHO MET TOGETHER IN
Jerusalem were Jews. This is an all-important fact, because
it explains why the Christian church did not inaugurate
an entirely new type of worship. With other Jews they
accepted the Old Testament as sacred scripture. The only
difference between Jewish Christians and their fellow
countrymen was the fact that they believed the Messiah
had come, while the rest waited for his coming in the
future. Jewish Christians believed that Jesus Christ was
the divine deliverer of Israel foretold by the prophets, and
were convinced that God had proved this conclusively by
raising Jesus from the dead and by empowering the young
Church with the Holy Spirit. This is, indeed, the theme
of the first Christian sermon, preached by Peter:

This Jesus did God raise up, whereof we all are witnesses.
Being therefore by the right hand of God exalted, and having
received of the Father the promise of the Holy Ghost, he hath
poured forth this which ye see and hear. (Acts 2:32-33.)

Both orthodox Jews and Christian Jews had, therefore,
been borne along a common Jewish river of religious
tradition, which became divided only by their differing
attitudes to our Lord. This difference of belief in regard
to Jesus did not at first involve the expulsion of Christian
Jews from the Jewish services. Hence the first Christians
did not think of themselves as the founders of a new faith.
The temple and the synagogue and their liturgies formed
the natural background of their worship.

19

Thus the first Christians in Jerusalem celebrated a Jewish liturgy with minor modifications. It was simply a revised version of the worship of the synagogue. And the synagogue had a twofold importance for the first generation of Christians. In the first place, our Lord and Paul carried on their ministries in the synagogues. After the temptation in the wilderness, Jesus went to the synagogue "as his custom was" (Luke 4:16). His greatest miracles of healing were accomplished there (Matt. 12:9; Mark 1:23; Luke 13:10). Some of his most famous words were spoken in the synagogue (Luke 4:18-27). Moreover, Paul, whenever he visited a new city, immediately made the synagogue the spearhead of his evangelistic advance.

The importance of the synagogue for our purpose is that its worship exerted a profound influence on the worship of the apostolic Church. The main elements of its worship were carried over into Christian services. The prayers, the praise, the reading of the Scriptures, and the exposition of them, were the fundamentals of Christian worship. Moreover, the worship of the synagogue was nonsacrificial in character, and it provided a place for a simple liturgy with responses, as well as extemporary prayers. Both these features were characteristic of apostolic worship.

The fact that the traditional Jewish structure of worship, with certain important additions, satisfied the first Christians, can be inferred from the scanty references to the details of worship that are given in the New Testament. The Jewish structure is assumed throughout, rendering it superfluous to describe the mode of worship in detail. Following the hints embedded in the fabric of the New Testament, it is possible to describe the essential features of apostolic worship.

1. *Praise*. There are many references in the New Testa-

ment to psalms, hymns, and spiritual songs. Like the Jews, the Christians would use the Psalter, the praisebook of the temple, to draw upon; but over and above this there are a number of fragments of hymns to be found in the New Testament. In I Tim. 3:16 we have a fragment of a hymn of praise to Christ. The book of Revelation has a number of such verses of hymns, notably 4:8, 11; 11:15-18; 14:7; 15:3, 4. These are clearly modeled in style and structure on the Psalms. Other definitely Christian fragments of hymns are also found in Rev. 5:9, 10; 12:10-12; 19:5, 6-8.

It was stated earlier that the chief difference between Christians and Jews was the fact that the former believed Christ to be the Messiah, while the latter regarded him as a blasphemer, a criminal, and an impostor. It is known that the hymns in the book of Revelation are distinctively Christian by the fact that many of them praise the Lamb who was slain, and glory in the cross of Christ. Other early hymns are the *Magnificat, Benedictus,* and *Nunc Dimittis.*

2. *Prayers.* These made up a large part of early Christian worship. A fairly comprehensive description of prayers and their subjects is given in I Tim. 2:1-2. The types of prayer commended are thanksgivings, supplications, and intercessions. It may also be supposed that the Lord's Prayer occupied an important position in their worship.

3. *The Scripture.* The reading and exposition of scripture was an important feature of their services. I Tim. 4:13 makes this evident, where the apostle Paul writes: "Till I come, give heed to reading, to exhortation, to teaching." From the vivid accounts of the Acts of the Apostles, we know how eagerly Paul seized every opportunity of preaching the Word in the synagogues of Asia Minor.

Thus far, our evidence demonstrates that Christian worship followed the lines laid down in the worship of the synagogue, by its threefold admixture of praise, prayers, scripture readings and exposition, with the addition of the Lord's Prayer and Christian hymns. It is also probable that the Christian service had some equivalent to the Jewish *Shema,* or creed. It has been suggested that the liturgical arrangment of Phil. 2:5-11 indicates that it was the creed of the church at Philippi. For these hints the apostolic Church was indebted to the synagogue, but at this point the resemblance ends.

4. *The Christian Sacraments.* These are distinctively Christian in origin and meaning. Our evidence for their use is, to take only two references, Rom. 6:3 for baptism, and I Cor. 11:23 ff. for the Lord's Supper. While there is in John's baptism a parallel for the Christian ceremony of initiation, the Lord's Supper is uniquely Christian.

Scholars, such as Rudolf Otto, hold that the *kiddush,* or Jewish family meal, was the framework of the Lord's Supper, but a more convincing and interesting theory is that put forward by Dom Gregory Dix in *The Shape of the Liturgy.*[1] He holds that the origin of the Last Supper is to be found in the *chabûrah,* or confraternity meal of Jewish religious brotherhoods. The *chabûrôth* were societies of friends gathered together for purposes of charity or devotion. Their corporate meeting took the form of a weekly supper, usually held on the eve of sabbaths or festivals.

The details of procedure are found in a document of A.D. 200, namely the *Berakoth* (Blessings) . This document incorporates the customs of the two preceding centuries. From this basis it is possible to reconstruct what probably happened in detail at the Last Supper.

No food, not even a relish, was eaten without a preliminary "blessing," or giving of thanks. After the relishes,

---

[1] Pp. 50 ff. Used by permission of A. & C. Black.

the guests all washed their hands, as in John's account of the eve of the Passion. After this point late-comers were not allowed to enter. Then followed a grace before the meal. This invariably took the following form: "Blessed be Thou, O Lord our God, eternal King, Who bringest forth bread from the earth." The blessing would be pronounced by the host or leader, as he took bread in his hands and broke it. After partaking of a fragment of it, he distributed a piece to each person at the table.

The meal itself followed this grace and each new kind of food was blessed by the leader in the name of all present each time it appeared. But, by exception, each time the wine-cup was refilled, each individual blessed it for himself with the words: "Blessed art Thou, O Lord our God, eternal King, Who createst the fruit of the vine." When the meal was concluded, an attendant brought round a basin and napkin, and hands were again washed.

Finally, the meal being ended, there came the "Benediction," or grace after meals. This was a lengthy prayer said by the leader representing all who had participated in the meal. On important occasions solemnity was added by reciting the prayer over a special cup of wine. This is, of course, the parallel to Paul's reference to "the cup of blessing" (I Cor. 10:16). When the Benediction was completed, the cup was sipped by the leader and then handed round to each of those present. Finally, the members sang a psalm and the meeting broke up.

A shortened form of this important prayer is as follows:

The host begins: "Let us give thanks."
The guests answer: "Blessed be the Name of the Lord from this time forth for evermore."
The host: "With the assent of those present— (they indicate

their assent) —we will bless Him of Whose bounty we have partaken."

The guests: "Blessed be He of Whose bounty we have partaken and through Whose goodness we live." [2]

After this preface, with responses, the host leads into a prayer of thanksgiving to God for his providence and lovingkindness. He thanks God for the deliverance out of Egypt, the giving of the law, "the life, grace and lovingkindness which Thou hast bestowed upon us, and for the food wherewith Thou dost constantly feed and sustain us."

The prayer then moves into petition and intercession for the people of Israel, the city of Jerusalem, the temple, and the physical needs of the worshipers.

In this *chabûrah* meal can be discerned the lineaments of the Lord's Supper. Our Lord takes bread and breaks it, giving the usual grace over it and distributing it to the disciples. But as he distributes it he says: "This is my body, which is for you: this do in remembrance of me" (I Cor. 11:24) . Thus he invests an old rite with a new significance. He is going to death the next evening and when the disciples next meet for a *chabûrah*, the action symbolizing his broken body will be pregnant with new meaning.

The next change in the normal ritual comes after Judas has left the company and the meal is over. The time has come for the rinsing of hands. Instead of leaving this menial task to the attendant or the youngest among them, He, their Lord, takes towel and basin and, with unforgettable humility, washes not only their hands but their feet.

Then, after much conversation, as the evening is getting late, it is time to conclude the meeting with the "Thanksgiving." It is said over a cup of wine. Jesus gives thanks, in

[2] *Ibid.,* pp. 52-53.

the traditional responsive prayer, and after this is ended, he distributes the cup to them. While the cup passes from one to another in silence, he makes a second startling pronouncement: "This cup is the new covenant in my blood: this do, as oft as ye drink it, in remembrance of me" (I Cor. 11:25). Thus was the *chabûrah* meal given a rich new meaning in connection with the death of the Lord.

This distinctively Christian act of worship, the Lord's Supper, was celebrated in private houses. It may be that the prayers, with the exception of the Lord's Prayer and the blessings, had not yet reached the fixity of liturgical form. The president would often pray extemporaneously. Christian worship was in a state of transition. Its forms did not crystallize until the fourth and fifth centuries.

Early Christian worship also contained two other elements: the "speaking with tongues" and the agape, or love feast. Evidence for the former comes from I Cor. 14. This form of ecstatic utterance apparently expressed the spontaneous elation of pagan converts to the Christian faith. Paul looks askance at this form of worship, not because of its irrepressible joy, but because of its unintelligibility. It does not lead to edification of the other members present at worship and is therefore found wanting.

The love feast was a communal meal, the ancient counterpart of the modern "church social." It appears to have preceded the Lord's Supper at Corinth and to have been the occasion of much gluttony and irreverence. These two elements of primitive Christian worship disappeared after the first century: the first probably because it fell under the apostle's displeasure, the second because it was abused.

CHAPTER 3

The Worship of the Eastern Orthodox Church

THE PASSING OF THREE OR FOUR CENTURIES SHOWS A GREAT alteration in the character of Christian worship. In the last chapter it was seen that the first Christians worshiped very much as their brothers, the Orthodox Jews. We picture them meeting in private houses for their celebration of the divine meal. There is no fixed order of worship. The form of the prayers is often free and is ordered by the presiding minister.

In the fourth century, worship is not celebrated in private houses, but in stately cathedrals and magnificent churches, not in free and simple forms of service, but in fixed and ordered worship.

How is the transformation to be accounted for? First, by the fact that conditions have changed. The Christian religion is no longer a prohibited and persecuted faith. The worshipers no longer meet in secret, ready to be hunted out by the imperial officers, and, if they will not recant, prepared to be sent to the arena in Rome to be mangled by the lions. It is no longer a "hole-and-corner" affair celebrated secretly in the upper room of a poor house in a side street. The Christian religion is now protected, even encouraged, by the Empire. The result is that Christians erect church buildings which excel in magnificence even the pagan temples; the officials of the faith are decked in splendid vestments; and public worship reflects the historical fact that the despised Nazarene has conquered the imperial might of Rome. This is, in fact, Christianity on parade.

In the second place, every age of adventure is followed by an era of reflection, pioneering by philosophy. The adventurers of England, e.g. Drake, Hawkins, and Raleigh, flourished in the sixteenth century; the philosophers of Britain, Lord Herbert of Cherbury, Bishop Berkeley, and David Hume, lived a century or more later. The age of the adventurous expansion of the Church among the Gentiles was followed by an age of reflection and meditation. The theologians had now come to understand more fully the meaning of the mighty acts of God in the incarnation, the cross, and the resurrection of Christ. These doctrines were carefully elaborated because they had to be protected from the misunderstandings of the heretics. They were built into a creed. There is no longer a recklessness about worship as in the days of Paul. Men trust rather to the careful statements of authority than to the direct inspiration of the Holy Spirit. The result is that worship becomes conservative in form and carefully ordered into a fixed liturgy.

A third feature of this liturgical worship is that it is shared or common worship. In the first services of the early Church the leader prayed and the people simply signified their approval by saying, "Amen." In the worship of the Eastern Orthodox Church, however, all Christians have a larger part to play in the worship. The set framework of the liturgy allows them to do this.

These, then, are the reasons for the production of a dignified, a beautiful, and an ordered liturgy. To save any possible confusion, it ought to be stated that there is not one, and only one, Orthodox liturgy (as there is only one Roman rite) ; there are, in fact, several Orthodox liturgies, but each is in the native tongue of the worshipers. There

27

are three liturgies of great importance: the liturgy of St. Basil, the liturgy of St. Chrysostom, and the liturgy of the Presanctified. The first two are rather similar, and the second is in effect a briefer version of the first and is now in general use among Orthodox Christians. The third is used only on the Wednesdays and Fridays of Lent.

What is this worship like? To appreciate the worship one must first understand something of the architecture. The Orthodox church is usually built in the shape of a cross or a ship. It has three main divisions which correspond to the three types of worshipers. The back or western end of the nave is kept free for beginners, learners and penitents; the central part of the nave is kept for the faithful (or, as we might call them, members or mature Christians). Both groups are separated from the priests by a magnificent screen, called the "iconostasis," on which icons, or flat images, are represented. Behind this great screen is the sanctuary where the priests say their prayers in secret. This sanctuary contains a Holy Table on which lie the Gospels—to symbolize the presence of the Lord Christ; a cross—to signify where the sacrifice is offered; and the holy gifts of bread and wine.

The iconostasis, or screen, has three doors. The central door is named the "Royal Door," the opening and shutting of which has a special symbolic meaning in the services. There are images of Christ and the Virgin Mary on either side of this door, and on the door itself is an image of the angel of God announcing to Mary that she should give birth to the Saviour of the world. There are also two other doors: one is the door for the deacon, who conducts the people's part of the service and who is a liaison officer between the people and the priests behind the screen. The other door is called the "Server's Door": this is used for two processions in the course of the liturgy, known as the "Great" and "Little" entrances.

We must now try to picture the service itself. In reality there are two services proceeding at the same time. The action of the priest or priests goes on behind the screen and, except for a few exclamations aloud, his prayers are offered in secret. The service begins with the *Prothesis,* by which is intended the elaborate preparation of the elements of bread and wine. Five small loaves are used by the priest to typify the five loaves of our Lord's miracle in the feeding of the multitude. Meanwhile, the reader leads the prayers of the people.

Then follows the *Service of the Catechumens,* or learners. This service is not unlike Anglican Matins or a Free Church morning service. It includes prayers, psalms, and scripture readings. After this preliminary, the deacon enters the choir to read the prayers, which are litanies requiring the responses of the people. When he has entered, all three doors of the screen are opened to symbolize the opening of the heavens at the baptism of Jesus. One quotation from these prayers will show their beautiful phrasing and their wide sympathy and comprehensiveness:

In peace let us make our supplication to the Lord:

For the peace that is from above and for the salvation of our souls;

For the peace of the whole world, the welfare of God's Holy Church, for the unity of all;

For this holy house, for those that in devotion, faith, and fear of God do enter therein;

For this city, for this holy church, for every city and land and for those who dwell in faith therein;

For healthful seasons, for abundance of the earth's fruits, and for peaceful days;

For those who travel by sea or land, for the sick and suffering, for those that are in bonds and their safety;

That we may be preserved from all tribulation, wrath, and necessity, assist, preserve, pity and keep us, O God, by Thy grace. . . .

With all the saints let us commend ourselves and each other and our lives unto Christ our God.

After these prayers are ended, we reach the first climax of the service. This is known as the Little Entrance. The deacon, bearing the Gospel Book, and the priest, come from the sanctuary into the nave, preceded by a reader carrying a lighted taper. This reminds the worshipers of Christ's entry with the divine gospel from the sanctuary of heaven into the darkness of the world. It is a vivid dramatic portrayal of the text, "I am the light of the world." Fittingly, there follows the reading of the Epistle and Gospel. This, in turn, is succeeded by a litany or responsive prayer for the catechumens. The homily, or sermon, has entirely disappeared. Then the catechumens are dismissed.

The third part of the service now begins. This is the *Liturgy of the Faithful*. After the prayers of the faithful, the hymn of the cherubim is sung, during which the Great Entrance takes place. In this procession all the clergy take part: the acolytes bear lights, thurifers swing the incense, and the other ministers carry replicas of our Saviour's passion—the cross, the spear, the scourge, and the thorns. The procession enters by the Server's Door and returns to the sanctuary through the Royal Door, enveloped in clouds of incense. Then the Royal Door is closed until the priest and deacon have made their communion. Then as the priest and deacon come through the Royal Door bearing the gifts of bread and wine to the faithful, the other two doors are flung open.

Following the Great Entrance there is a noble prayer of consecration, beginning with the *Sursum Corda* ("Lift up your hearts"), continuing with the *Sanctus* ("Holy, Holy, Holy"), following with a thanksgiving for God's revelation to and redemption of man, including the words of institution, and the epiclesis, or prayer that the Holy Spirit may so consecrate the bread and wine that they may convey the most sacred benefits of Christ's sacrifice to the assembled faithful. Then the people receive their communion, both adults and children, as is the custom. The prayer of thanksgiving follows, concluding with the petition:

So that this life ended in the hope of life eternal, I may come into that everlasting rest where the voices of those who keep high festival shall never cease, and where the beatitude of those who behold the ineffable beauty of Thy countenance is infinite.

The service ends with a dismissal of the faithful.

What are the striking characteristics of this form of worship? First, the element of mystery and the symbolism. The whole service is a holy drama taking place in heaven and on earth. It is not only concerned with the sacrifice of Christ; that is seen in its proper perspective as one great event in a series of events that accomplished our salvation. The drama begins in heaven and shows the eternal Son of God coming to earth, being baptized, crucified, and rising again. The sanctuary symbolizes heaven, the nave earth. The entrances show the condescension of the Incarnation, Christ's humility in laying aside his heavenly privileges in coming to earth.

The bringing in of the Gospel in a solemn procession, preceded by lights, represents the Saviour's coming into the world, and his illumination of the ignorance and sin that are darkness. The Book itself manifests the presence

31

of the incarnate Lord. The *Sanctus* is the reply of the congregation to the angelic *Gloria in Excelsis;* the Response corresponds to the prophecies of the Old Testament, as does the Epistle with the witness of the Apostles. David's attestation to "great David's greater Son" is the Alleluia. The first phase of the service comes to its climax in the Reading of the Gospel.

The second phase of worship uses the gifts of bread and wine to represent the Lord's presence. The Holy Table symbolizes Christ's sepulcher, while the linen corporal stands for the cloth enveloping his body. The veil of the paten represents the kerchief surrounding his head. The larger veil or aer, which covers both chalice and paten, recalls the stone with which Joseph shut the sepulcher. The Great Entrance is the procession which re-enacts the way of the cross, while the placing of the chalice and paten on the altar re-enacts the burial. The consecration corresponds to the resurrection.

Thus the first and outstanding characteristic of this form of worship is the sense of mystery, appropriate to a great revelation of God.

The second feature is the immense importance and emphasis given to the resurrection and ascension of our Lord. If the Western Church concentrates on the Cross, the means of grace, the Eastern Church concentrates on the end of grace, eternal life.

In the third place, compared with the simple and concentrated prayers of the West, the prayers of the East are highly imaginative and poetic. In them the soul of the worshiper takes wings. One instance may be given.

Son of God, receive me as a partaker in Thy Mystical Supper. For not as a secret enemy do I approach, not with the kiss of Judas, but as the thief will I confess Thee. Remember me, O Lord, in Thy Kingdom. I am not worthy, Lord, that Thou shouldest come unto me, but as Thou wast content to lodge in the stall of brute beasts and in the house of Simon the leper, and didst receive the harlot, a sinner like unto me, vouchsafe in like manner to enter into the stable of my brutish soul, my defiled body dead in sin and spiritually leprous, and as Thou didst not disdain the mouth of the harlot when she kissed Thee, disdain not me, O Lord my God, but make me worthy to partake of Thy most Holy Body and Blood.

The fourth characteristic of this form of worship is that there is a place for devout silence. The images are the aids to worshiping God. Moreover, Christ our exemplar is in every stage of his life, from babyhood to manhood, from incarnation to resurrection, brought before the worshiper's eyes by icons and processions. The eye is well as the voice is engaged in worshiping God.

What defects are there in this deeply biblical worship? The chief is surely the absence of instruction. There is neither sermon nor homily. This means that the worship is always beautiful, but it must often be unintelligible to the uninstructed. Also, this type of worship does not send a man out dissatisfied with the world and with himself, for the prophetic note is missing.

It may be suggested that there is an excess of symbolism in the services. This is particularly the case when we consider that the holy bread is elaborately divided with ceremonial, each piece being dedicated to some person of the Holy Trinity, or of the apostles. Unless the congregation is thoroughly instructed the ceremonial will be almost meaningless. As it is, the service is overweighted with symbolism. Often the congregation are spectators rather than participants in worship.

CHAPTER 4

The Worship of the Roman Catholic Church

IN THE FIRST FEW CENTURIES OF CHRISTIAN WORSHIP EACH important Christian center had its own order of worship. From the years A.D. 500 to A.D. 900, however, there were two main rites in the Western Church, the Gallican or French rites and the Roman. The Roman order of worship was at first confined to the local use of the city of Rome, while the Gallican rites spread over the rest of Europe and varied very much according to local usage. At the end of the period the Roman rite gained the ascendancy, but in the intervening years the Roman rite had been influenced greatly by the Gallican rites. It was not finally fixed in form until 1570, but since then it has remained practically unchanged.

If you were to go from an Eastern Orthodox service to a Roman Catholic celebration of worship, at first sight they might appear similar. They both have the same structure: a Liturgy of the Word (a service, known in the East as the "Liturgy of the Catechumens") followed by the Liturgy of the Upper Room (a communion service, known in the East as the "Liturgy of the Faithful"). This is not in the least surprising, as these two services retain the division which was found in the apostolic Church. The Liturgy of the Word corresponds to the synagogue service, while the Liturgy of the Upper Room is the counterpart to the primitive Lord's Supper. You would find in both the use of set prayers, vestments, and the division between the nave and the sanctuary, and other similarities.

On the other hand, you would also discover a great difference in emphasis. Eastern worship, you will recall, is a Christian mystery re-enacting the divine descent to earth for the purpose of conveying eternal life to the human race. Western worship, by contrast, is the drama of the great Sacrifice. The East stresses the Incarnation, and its focal center is Bethlehem. The West stresses the Atonement, and its focal center is Calvary. The theology of the East is taken from John's Gospel, with special emphasis on its prologue (ch. 1) ; the theology of the West is Pauline, and finds its expression in the apostle's epistles.

Another contrast is seen in the prevailing spirit of worship. If the East is mystical in character, the West is precise and practical. This difference in atmosphere is conveyed by the respective prayers. The Eastern Orthodox prayers are looser in structure, lengthier, and more imaginative. The Western prayers are compact and definite in their petitions. This can be tested by comparing the prayer of the priest in the Orthodox liturgy offered up after receiving Communion with any collect in the Roman rite.

It would seem as if the dominant aim of worship is different in the two liturgies. Eastern worshipers long for release from the world and their desire is for eternal life. Western worshipers, on the other hand, long for release from sin, and their desire is for righteousness. The Easterner looks to the future; the Westerner to the present.

The complications of the modern rite would require a lengthy explanation, but some idea of the movement of Roman worship can be given by studying the simpler structure of the Roman rite as it was celebrated about the year A.D. 450. One advantage of studying the Roman rite in its earlier form is that it expresses the genius of Roman worship more truly than does the later rite. We have the authority of a great Roman liturgiologist for this view.

Those very things which in the popular mind are considered distinctive of Romanism, and which go to make up in the main what people call the sensuousness of the Roman rite, form precisely the element in it which is not originally Roman at all, but has been gradually borrowed, adopted in the course of the ages. The genius of the native Roman rite is marked by simplicity, practicality, a great sobriety and self-control, gravity and dignity.[1]

This was its structure in the middle of the fifth century:

I. THE LITURGY OF THE WORD.

Introit by two choirs as the clergy enter.

Kyries (3).

Celebrant's Salutation.

Collect.

Old Testament Reading.

Antiphonal Chant.

Reading from Epistles.

Gradual (psalm chanted as solo).

Alleluia.

Reading from the Gospels (including entry with lights, responses by worshipers and incense).

Dismissal of those not communicating.

II. THE LITURGY OF THE UPPER ROOM.

Offertory: collection of elements, preparation of elements for Communion, offering of gifts and admixture, while a psalm is sung.

Salutation and *Sursum corda.*

Prayer of Consecration:—

Preface,

Proper Preface,

Sanctus,

Canon (center of prayer).

Kiss of Peace.

Breaking of Bread.

Lord's Prayer.

Communion (Celebrant first, then people, during singing of psalm).

Collect of Thanksgiving.

Dismissal by Deacon.

[1] Edmund Bishop, *Liturgica Historica* (New York: Oxford University Press, 1918).

Later additions increased the splendor of the ceremonial. But in this early rite there was little ceremonial. For instance, there was no elevation of the Host during the words of institution, which is the climax of the present Roman service. Further, censing, bell-ringing, and lights were excluded. There was elaborate ceremonial only at the entry of the celebrant and during the singing of the Gospel lection.

Now what was the main purpose of the Roman communion service? Its intention was to re-enact what our Lord did by anticipation in the Last Supper. When our Lord instituted the Last Supper, he had yet to offer himself upon the cross as "a ransom for many," but his blessing of the bread and the wine, as symbols of his body and blood, clearly pointed to the consummation of the Cross. The Roman Communion aims to re-present the sacrifice upon the cross. Its method is to use as nearly as possible our Lord's own words and actions, so that the bread and wine are "transubstantiated" (changed into the body and blood of Christ). They believe that the appearance remains the same, but that the underlying substance has changed. It is not a magical change performed by the priest; it is a miracle wrought by God. The prayer of consecration is succeeded by the sacrifice, when Christ the holy victim is offered with a prayer for the acceptance of the worshipers. This is the prime intention of the Mass.

There seem to be four outstanding merits in the Roman rite. First, what we may call its *objectivity*. There is no reference to the moods of the worshipers; the emphasis is entirely upon God and what he has accomplished and can accomplish. In the second place, the Roman rite has *universality*. The liturgy is celebrated almost entirely in the Latin tongue in every Roman Catholic church the world over. Moreover, the wording is identical, with a few outstanding exceptions, in every local church. The Roman Catholic believer, therefore, feels at home in whatever country he may worship, as soon as he enters a Catholic church.

A third advantage of the Roman service is the *simplicity and sobriety of the prayers*. They are clearly understood and they keep strictly to the end they have in view. The typical Roman prayer is the collect with its brief invocation and petition concluding, "Through Jesus Christ our Lord."

A fourth characteristic is the *variety* within the unity. The Eastern Orthodox liturgy has little variety. The Roman liturgy has variable parts, which change according to the Christian year. This attempt to relate the mighty acts of God in Christ to the Christian life is a major achievement. The great drama of salvation starts in the season of Advent with the preparation for the coming Messiah to his chosen people in the Old Testament, and prepares the believer to receive Christ in his heart. The Christmas services celebrate the Incarnation, and through the coming of the Christ child womanhood and babyhood are sanctified. In the season of Lent the Christian relates the temptations in the wilderness and the victory of our Lord over them to his own life, striving to overcome them in the same power. The cross and the glorious resurrection are also commemorated, the first with befitting sadness and the second with solemn joy. They remind Christians to die to sin and rise with newness of life. Then follows the celebration of the founding of the Church at Whitsuntide, with its emphasis on the need of the cleansing and illuminating Spirit in the Christian life. And various red-letter days in the calendar remind the Christian of the example of the saints and martyrs. The whole Christian year is an attempt, and a successful one, to relate the wide sweep of the Incarnation to the day-to-day life of the individual believer.

Fifth, a due importance is given to the *centrality of the sacrifice of Christ* and the need for our sacrifice in response.

What, then, are the defects of this rite? Chief among them is the emphasis on the propitiatory character of the Mass—the suggestion, that is, that God's just wrath is appeased by the offering of this sacrifice. This led to all kinds of abuses, as the Mass was regarded as a magical means of obtaining a boon and a way of freeing souls from the torments of purgatory. Friedrich Heiler says bluntly in condemnation, "The purchased private Mass is the cancer in the Roman system of services." [2]

The same emphasis on the miracle performed, reaching its climax in the elevation of the Host, tended to make the gathered congregation mere spectators and not participants in the service, united to their Lord and to one another. Evelyn Underhill has written that the Mass "encouraged utilitarian religion by concentrating attention on a miracle performed and witnessed, and a benefit obtained." [3]

Liturgical experts are agreed, also, that the present Canon of the Mass is a patchwork of prayers from different ages that do not fit in with one another. It has no orderly progression and parts of it are ambiguous, if not unintelligible. A further weakness is the absence of a prayer for the Holy Spirit to consecrate both the worshipers and the elements.

[2] *The Spirit of Worship,* tr. W. Montgomery (New York: George H. Doran Co., 1926).
[3] *Op. cit.*

A further objection can rightly be made to the static quality of the Mass. It has remained unaltered since 1570; its language is still archaic and for the simple worshipers it often remains unintelligible. It is true that they are supplied with copies of the missal, with the Latin on one side and their native tongue opposite; but the objection still stands that for the most part the worship is offered in a dead language. This is bound to encourage superstition among unlearned folk. It results in the experience which Tennyson described in the words of the farmer:

> An' I hallus coom'd to's choorch, afoor
>   moy Sally wur dead,
> An' 'eärd 'um a bummin' awaäy, loike a
>   buzzard-clock ower my 'eäd,
> An' I niver knaw'd whot a meän'd but
>   I thowt a 'ad summut to saäy,
> An' I thowt a said whot a owt to 'a
>   said, an' I coom'd awaäy.[4]

Because Roman worship is offered in a strange tongue, it lacks one of the essential marks of true worship: edification—the building up of the faith of the worshipers.

[4] "Northern Farmer: Old Style."

CHAPTER 5

Lutheran Worship

"THE REFORMATION ACCORDING TO THE WORD OF GOD," which gave rise to the various Protestant churches, was an attempt to purify medieval Catholicism by a return to the doctrines, the polity, the Christian way of life, and the worship of the primitive Church. It may be said to have taken three main forms. The one was conservative, which issued in the Lutheran Communion and the Anglican or Episcopalian Church, and, two centuries later, in the formation of the daughter church of the Anglican Communion, the Methodist Church. The second form was moderate, which produced the Calvinist churches known as Presbyterian or Reformed. The third, more radical form of the Reformation movement founded the Independent churches (whether of the Baptist or Congregational persuasions) and the Quakers, or Society of Friends. Among these three families of Protestant churches, the line cannot be drawn rigidly since the Congregationalists, for example, are Calvinists theologically and should be classed as a type of Reformed worship, but for their theory of the "gathered church" and their espousal of free forms of prayer at a time when Presbyterians preferred a set liturgy. Similarly, the Methodists, though founded under God by a loyal Anglican priest, John Wesley, combine the Anglican tradition in Holy Communion with the use of free prayers in their Sunday services in the Puritan tradition. Then, again, the Quakers are even more radical than the Baptists in their reordering of worship and rejection of forms. Our concern will be to show that in their variety each of the

41

Protestant traditions—conservative, moderate, and radical —has a valuable contribution to make to the worship and witness of the whole church of Christ.

The Lutheran churches derive from the beginning of the Reformation in 1517 when Martin Luther, a devout Augustinian monk, who had failed to find peace by trying to earn his salvation with good works, discovered that he was justified by faith in the all-sufficiency of Christ's work. As a result he began to strip off the barnacles which were impeding the advance of the ark of salvation, the Church. This he did most dramatically in challenging the sale of indulgences or pardons and asserting the free remission of sins given in the gospel, by nailing his *Ninety-five Theses* on the door of the castle church in Wittenberg. The large and vigorous Lutheran churches, of which he is the father under God, are strongest in Germany, in the Scandinavian countries, and in the United States.

Revolutionary as were the effects of Luther's challenge of the western Catholic Church, his intention was not to create a new gospel or a new church, but rather to free the old gospel from the new shackles of later medieval corruptions. His plans for liturgical reform were contained in two treatises. The *Formulary of the Mass and Communion* was produced in December, 1523, in which his aim was to retain as much of the medieval Mass as was not contradicted by the teachings of the Bible. His second work, *The German Mass and Order of Divine Service,* was less conservative, in that it provided for the celebration of Holy Communion in German, the language of the common people of his nation. Its chief features, apart from the vernacular emphasis, were as follows: the provision of German hymns to be sung by the congregation (replacing the elaborate polyphonic Latin praise hitherto sung by the choir alone); the evident intention throughout that the people should be instructed in the meaning of the gospel, both in the readings and preaching of the Word, as well as in the representation of the drama of our redemption in the Holy Communion. Its paramount importance was that it preserved, at least in the sixteenth century, the unity of the Liturgy of the Word and the Liturgy of the Upper Room. This unity was, however, lost in the seventeenth and eighteenth centuries, partly because the Thirty Years' War interrupted church life, partly because Lutherans tended to be influenced by later Calvinistic depreciation of the Communion, and partly because under the influence of rationalism, the sermon came to displace worship in importance, as the pulpit came to dominate the altar, and an inner piety was too ready to disparage tradition and the sacraments as if they were mere external forms and ultimately unnecessary. During the past eight or nine decades, however, there has been a welcome return to an appreciation of classical and historical Lutheran worship, with its unity of ante-Communion and Communion, the Liturgy of the Word and the Liturgy of the Upper Room, as the pattern for Sunday worship.[1] If a non-Lutheran were to enter an American Lutheran church sympathetically and share in the service, what would his chief impressions be? He could not fail to notice certain distinctive qualities about this type of worship.

First, it would be evident that it is a liturgical or set type of service of great dignity, which is also marvelously joyous. As a liturgical type of service it offers the worshiper many opportunities through versicles and responses to share in the prayers, not merely in the praise. In brief, it

[1] Luther D. Reed, *The Lutheran Liturgy* (Philadelphia: Muhlenberg Press, 1947), p. 585.

is liturgical and also lyrical. To this day Luther's sense of glad liberation from the thraldom of sin, guilt, suffering, and death, throbs through the Common Service, as it is called in American Lutheran churches. Allied with this is a strong sense of fellowship. This is a people's service in which the community of the redeemed in Christ, the forgiven and justified in him, unite in a common experience and in a language understood by the people. This service has been described as "a romantic expression of living Christian experience." [2] At the same time this community is also based upon a common understanding of truth, the revelation of God in history—in patriarchs, lawgivers, prophets, apostles, and supremely, in the incarnation, the passion, and the resurrection of Christ. Yet the revelation that is made of God's character and activities which evokes the response of adoring faith issues from mystery and never loses its sense of the infinitude and transcendence of God. As Luther never tired of saying, the Hidden God it is who is revealed. Thus the didactic or intellectual element never excludes the aspiring, unitive, mystical desire of the soul. And nowhere is this more clear than in the Communion itself, where—without any precise intellectual definition, for that would dissipate mystery as the sun the mists—there is a sense of the real presence of Christ. To surmise that there is a despising of the intellect would be erroneous; for the lessons, the preaching, the Creed, all testify to its importance. Similarly, the ethical concern is there in the Prayer of Confession, as in the Ten Commandments. If this rich and complex worship, combining traditional elements and personal experience, linking revelation in the Word-made-flesh to a Christian response in terms of

[2] *Our Heritage in Public Worship* (New York: Charles Scribner's Sons, 1935), p. 180.

heart, mind, and will, can be defined in one sentence, then D. H. Hislop almost succeeds. He maintains: "It is the Word revealed in human experience which is the Lutheran outlook, just as the Word revealed in Sovereign Will is the Calvinist approach." [3] The further point should be made that, as in an Episcopalian service, there is considerable variety between "high" and "low" ceremonial. As Heiler says: "The Lutheran Service can equally well assume the ornate robe of an elaborate liturgy, or the simplest dress of a Bible-reading." [4] Furthermore, the Lutherans (to whom Bach belongs) have always venerated music as a handmaid of worship.

No liturgy, far less the freer forms of worship, is immune from criticism. It has been urged against the Lutheran rite that it still bears the marks of its sixteenth-century origin in its reaction away from a false conception of sacrifice, so that the necessary element of sacrifice, the one oblation of Christ, and the oblation of his church, is relegated to a very minor position in the rite. It has also been suggested that the emphasis is too individualistic and insufficiently corporate, but that is mitigated if not entirely refuted by the sense of the present community, even if the deeper meaning of the communion of saints past as well as present has to be inferred from the *Tersanctus,* rather than explicitly understood in a prayer that commemorates the blessed who died in the faith. Some have contended that the prophetic note is rarely heard in Lutheran sermons. But these criticisms are, if true judgments, no reason for failing to appreciate the rich devotion and spiritual culture of which the Common Service has been so conspicuous a channel in Lutheran piety.

[3] *Ibid.,* p. 165.
[4] *Op. cit.*

The present Lutheran service can be divided into three parts.[5] The first is the Preparatory Confession; the second, the Office of the Word (corresponding in the ancient Church to the Liturgy of the Word intended for the catechumens) ; and the third, the Office of Holy Communion (corresponding to the Liturgy of the Upper Room in the ancient Church). After a triune invocation, the minister invites the congregation to confession, to which they respond in the versicles appropriate to the theme. The actual Confession of Sins follows, with an ensuing Prayer for Grace. The first part concludes with the minister making a declaration of grace, assuring the congregation and himself that God "hath had mercy upon us."

The second part begins with psalmody, then follows with the Introit (which strikes the keynote of the season or day of the Christian year) , and in turn there come the *Kyries* (or, cries for the help of God and Christ) and the exclamations of adoration called the *Gloria in Excelsis* (the song of the angels that greeted the infant Incarnate Lord) . The instructional part of the service moves toward its climax of the Sermon by way of the Salutation and Response ("The Lord be with you"—"And with thy spirit") , the Collect (short prayer) for the Day, the Epistle for the Day, the Gradual (some phrases from the Psalms as a transition from the epistle to the next item) , the Gospel for the Day, and the Creed (which is the Church's echo to the Word proclaimed in the gospel) . The Sermon is preached and the inevitable response of the people is in their offerings, in the General Prayer in which they have their repeated response after each paragraph, and in the Hymn.

The third part of the service, the Office of Holy Com-

[5] See the analysis of Reed, *op. cit.*, pp. 235-36.

munion, is itself subdivided into three sections: the Preface, the Consecration and Administration, and the Post (or After) Communion. The Preface consists of the Salutation, the *Sursum Corda* ("Lift up your hearts"), The Eucharistic (or Thanksgiving) Prayer, the Proper Preface (appropriate to the season of the Christian year, remembering different aspects of the Church's life in Christ, such as: Advent, Lent, Easter, Pentecost), and the *Sanctus* ("Holy, Holy, Holy"). The part of the service concentrating on the Consecration and Administration begins with the Lord's Prayer, continues with the warrant for the communion (the Words of Institution), the peace, the *Agnus Dei* ("O Christ, Thou Lamb of God, that takest away the sin of the world . . ."), until the distribution of the bread and wine is made at the chancel to the kneeling recipients. The bread is given with the words, "Take and eat, this is the Body of Christ, given for thee," and the wine with the words, "Take and drink, this is the Blood of the New Testament, shed for thy sins." When both sacred elements have been received, the minister says: "The Body of our Lord Jesus Christ and His precious Blood strengthen and preserve you in true faith unto everlasting life." The Blessing fittingly follows.

The climax having been reached, the After-Communion draws quietly and serenely to its close in the *Nunc Dimittis* (Simeon's Song), the Thanksgiving Prayer, the Salutation and *Benedicamus* ("Bless we the Lord"—Response: "Thanks be to God"), and the final Benediction (Aaronic).

It will have been noticed that there is throughout a rhythm of divine descent and the human aspiring ascent, which is the response that the revelation of God elicits in man.

CHAPTER 6

Anglican or Episcopalian Worship

IT IS THE CHIEF GLORY OF EPISCOPAL WORSHIP THROUGH THE
various Prayer Books of the Anglican Communion that
this is the only vernacular rite of the sixteenth century
which has remained substantially the same up to the
present day, and that its felicitous language is known and
loved not only in England, the land of its origin, but
throughout the United States and the British Commonwealth of Nations. Furthermore, its influence has been
great on the recent liturgical revival in the Presbyterian
churches of Scotland and America, and was significant in
the formative years of that now large and independent
daughter of Anglicanism, the Methodist Church. Congregationalists, for all their historic preference for free prayer,
have not remained untouched by its influence. The first
Unitarian liturgies, moreover, were doctrinal revisions of
the *Book of Common Prayer*.[1]

The importance of the Prayer Book is that it was
originally an attempted reconciliation of two types of
worship: the traditional (chiefly Roman, but partly Eastern) and the Reformed. The Episcopalians have worshiped
in this way, with few major changes, ever since 1549 when
Archbishop Cranmer introduced the first Book of Common
Prayer. The result is that this excellent liturgy, which
belongs to the time when the English reformers were re-
vising the worship of the Roman rite, incorporates both
the Roman conception of worship as the sacrificial offering

[1] See Alexander E. Peaston, *The Prayer Book Reform Movement in the
XVIIIth Century* (Oxford, Eng.: Basil Blackwell, 1940).

48

of corporate prayer and praise to God, and the Reformation conception of worship as the gathering of the congregation to hear the reading and exposition of the oracles of God. In the Episcopalian rite there is, therefore, a combination and balance of the downward movement of revelation through lesson, sermon, and sacrament, and the upward movement of aspiring devotion.

In compiling the first Prayer Book, Cranmer had at his disposal two sets of sources, the one traditional, the other contemporary. The Roman sources that he employed were several "uses" of the rite in England, such as those of Sarum (his chief source the liturgy at Salisbury Cathedral), Hereford, Bangor, York, and Lincoln, and the revised Breviary of Cardinal Quignonez, which had been produced in 1536 with papal approval. The main contemporary source that he used was the *Pious Consultation* put forth by the Reformed Archbishop of Cologne, Hermann von Wied, who was assisted by Melanchthon and Bucer. This was published in 1534.

From the Sarum, and other cathedral variations of the Roman rite, the devotional riches of the collects of the medieval church entered the *Book of Common Prayer*. From Quignonez, Cranmer compiled the lections and Psalms for Matins and Evensong. Morning Prayer was the result of fusing the orders of service from the monastic and secular offices for Matins, Lauds, and Prime. Similarly, the Breviary offices for Vespers and Compline were combined to produce Evening Prayer. Von Wied's influence may be found in the Invitatory Sentences, the Confession, the Absolution, and the Comfortable Words in the service of Holy Communion.

The influence of the Reformers was also seen in various other ways, notably in the translation from Latin into

English, in the rejection of the doctrine of transubstantiation (but without the denial of the Real Presence), in the simpler ceremonial, in the insistence that the laity should communicate, in the omission of legendary material from the lections, and, above all, in the position of honor given to the Bible as the Word of God. In almost all of these changes, Cranmer had been forestalled by Luther.

The result of the flowing together of these streams of worship was to produce a rite of great dignity, rich in historic tradition and beauty, in language that is lapidary, chaste, moving, but never effusive. Indeed, it can fairly be said that its translations, in some instances, improve upon the originals. That many generations have desired no better formulary of devotion can be proved by its survival and widespread use today among all the English-speaking peoples.

The story of the successive editions of the Prayer Book must be briefly told. It was revised in 1552 and again in a more conservative direction in 1662, after the convulsion of the Commonwealth was succeeded by the restoration of the monarchy, and it bore the influence of Archbishop Laud's hand in the fine Scottish book of 1637 which he had tried to foist on the stubbornly Presbyterian Scots. This influence and that of the Nonjurors, who would not recant their oath of allegiance to the Stuarts when William and Mary succeeded to the throne, who also delved into the history of the worship of the Eastern Orthodox churches, produced a greatly enriched communion service which has never been incorporated into the English Prayer Book (partly due to the State establishment of the Church of England), but which is substantially that of the American Prayer Book of 1789, and of its successive revisions of 1892 and 1928. Indeed, this structure of the American

Protestant Episcopal Church Communion which comes in part from the Eastern Church by way of Scotland is one of its chief glories.

What are the chief emphases in Episcopalian worship? It is rightly described as *Common Prayer* for a large proportion of the service is given to devotions, and these are not individualistic prayers but the corporate or common offerings of the whole church. The biblical or revelational element also is strong in the singing of Psalms, in the canticles, in the lections, and in the sermon (if of expository type). The third characteristic is, of course, the chief justification of a liturgy: that the set prayers with their responses give so large a vocal part to the worshiping people, who are made aware that numberless others are joining in this same service in other parts of the world, and the thrill of tradition links them with their forefathers in the faith. The austerely structured collects, with their balance of cadence, have unforgettable phrasing, as in the Collect for Purity, or in the Collect for the Sunday next before Easter commonly known as Palm Sunday. Other jewels of lambent phrase are, for example: "whose service is perfect freedom," describing the life of Christian obedience, or "among all the changes and chances of this mortal life," which expresses the mutability of an entirely this-worldly existence.[2]

Just as a preaching service (not the Ante-Communion completed by the Communion Service) came to be the most commonly frequented type of service in Lutheranism, so Matins, instead of a combined service uniting the Liturgy of the Word and the Liturgy of the Upper Room,

---

[2] These improve even upon the concentrated Latin they paraphrase; respectively, *qui servare regnare est* and *inter omnes viae et vitae huius varietatis.*

came to be the norm of Episcopal worship. This church, too, is concerned to return to the richer pattern of its earliest days, as is the Lutheran.

Criticisms can be made even of this admirable rite. The "Anglican Compromise," it must be acknowledged, has led to much doctrinal confusion where Roman, Calvinist, and Zwinglian interpretations of the Communion, for example, are possible. It is admitted that the Prayer of Humble Access is evidence of a soaring mysticism, but sobriety and dignity seem to characterize the rite rather than that glowing adoration distinctive of the Eastern Orthodox services. It has also been urged that the primary emphasis on prayer has often led to a lack of appreciation for the sermon, which has rarely been prophetic, and has sometimes degenerated into a mere moral homily, though this is less rare today. Others have accused the rite of encouraging an aesthetic escapism, a flight from the reality of contemporary life. But such have usually been either inveterate activists unaware of the need for meditation in our crowded and hurried life, or color-blind iconoclasts who recognize the beauty of holiness but are insensitive to the holiness of beauty.

An analysis of the American Protestant Episcopal Church Order for Holy Communion will enable the reader to have a more comprehensive view of this rich and profound form of worship:

The Approach	Lord's Prayer
and	Collect for Purity
Conditions	Decalogue, *Kyrie,* Summary, and Collect
of	Collect of Day
Admission	Epistle
	Gospel

	Creed
	Sermon
	Offertory
	Prayer for the Church
More Intimate	Exhortations
Approach	Invitation
	Confession
	Absolution
	Comfortable Words
Consummation	*Sursum Corda*
	Prefaces
	Sanctus
	Prayer of Humble Access
in	Words of Institution
	Oblation of elements
	Invocation
Oblation	Oblation of the worshipers
and Communion	Communion
and in	Lord's Prayer
	Thanksgiving
Adoration.	*Gloria in Excelsis*
	Blessing.[3]

It would be unfitting to conclude before giving examples of the sublimity of two of the prayers. The Prayer of Humble Access reads thus:

We do not presume to come to this thy Table, O merciful

[3] For the analysis I am indebted to R. D. Richardson (formerly principal of Ripon Hall, Oxford), editor of *The Harborne Liturgy,* and to Massey H. Shepherd, author of the admirable *Oxford American Prayer Book Commentary* (New York: Oxford University Press, 1950).

Lord, trusting in our own righteousness, but in thy manifold and great mercies. We are not worthy so much as to gather up the crumbs under thy Table. But thou art the same Lord, whose property is always to have mercy: Grant us, therefore, gracious Lord, so to eat the flesh of thy dear Son Jesus Christ, and to drink his blood, that our sinful bodies may be made clean by his body, and our souls washed through his most precious blood, and that we may evermore dwell in him, and he in us. *Amen.*

The Palm Sunday Collect reads:

Almighty and everlasting God, who, of thy tender love towards mankind, hast sent thy Son, our Saviour Jesus Christ, to take upon him our flesh, and to suffer death upon the cross, that all mankind should follow the example of his great humility; Mercifully grant, that we may both follow the example of his patience, and also be made partakers of his resurrection; through the same Jesus Christ our Lord. *Amen.*

Here, in short, is a worship in which mind, heart, and will are moved to faith, adoration, and service.

CHAPTER 7

Presbyterian and Methodist Worship

THE FIRST MOMENTUM OF THE REFORMATION PRODUCED THE
Lutheran and Anglican churches with their liturgical type
of worship, which is essentially conservative in character.
The second phase of the Reformation is associated chiefly
with the name of John Calvin and the city of Geneva, from
which his ministers went out to establish Presbyterian or
Reformed churches in France, Holland, Germany, Czecho-
slovakia, Scotland, and thence to the North American
continent in the ensuing centuries. In comparison with the
Lutheran and Anglican reformations, which were conservative, his type of churchmanship and worship may
seem radical, but it was considerably less so than that of the
Puritans in England and the Quakers, so that it may be
termed moderate as a mediating though logical view of
worship. Whereas Luther was willing to retain all features
of the medieval rite that did not conflict with the understanding of the gospel he obtained from the New Testament, Calvin held that what was not prescribed by the
Bible was positively forbidden to the Christian man. For
this reason, although his forms of worship attempted to
imitate the worship of the primitive Church, he was
primarily concerned to design a form of worship with
strong biblical authority.

Calvin's first rite took shape when he was minister of
the congregation of French exiles in Strasbourg between
1538 and 1541. He called the service book he translated
from Bucer's revision of the German rite in Strasbourg,
The Form of Prayers and Manner of Ministering the

Sacraments According to the Use of the Ancient Church. This was also to serve as the basis of his Genevan rite that appeared in 1542 and may be regarded as the parent of all Presbyterian and Reformed rites, For instance, the first Scottish Presbyterian rite, known as John Knox's Genevan Service Book, is substantially Calvin's.[1] It is of interest to note that Calvin had prepared a liturgy, a *set order of worship* in Geneva, although Reformed worship today is chiefly thought of as favoring free prayers; this was an innovation which was largely due to those errant Calvinists, the English Puritans, and dates from the *Directory of Public Worship* of 1644, advising ministers on how to conduct worship rather than providing them with set forms of worship. The influence of the Puritans lives on in Methodist worship and in the worship of the Baptists and Congregationalists and their affiliated bodies. Calvin's, it is worth repeating, was a set order of worship, as was also the work of the great English Presbyterian divine, Richard Baxter's *Reformed Liturgy* of 1660.

What are the leading characteristics of classical Calvinist worship? The atmosphere of Calvinist worship is a profound sense of abasement before the sovereign will of the high God. The transcendent and mysterious God in his inscrutable majesty is faced by finite man, who can pay him only the homage of obedience. This austere conception of worship is expressed typically in the Scottish metrical paraphrase of the Hundredth Psalm:

> All people that on earth do dwell,
> Sing to the Lord with cheerful voice;

[1] See W. D. Maxwell, *John Knox's Genevan Service Book, 1556* (Edinburgh: Oliver & Boyd, Ltd., 1931).

> Him serve with mirth, His praise forth tell,
> Come ye before Him and rejoice.
>
> Know that the Lord is God indeed;
> Without our aid He did us make;
> We are His folk, He doth us feed,
> And for His sheep He doth us take.

The paraphrase expresses the creatureliness of mankind, our utter dependence upon God ("Without our aid He did us make") ; and our duty as the elect, the chosen flock, is the obedience that he wills. In such worship we almost whisper, "To God alone be the glory."

It is a service which gives the written record of the revelation of God a high and dominating place. As Mitchell Hunter says: "The central place occupied by the Mass in the services of the Roman Church was taken by the Sermon in those of the Reformed; teaching was the preacher's great business, the service was indeed often called the preaching." [2] To Luther the Bible is the Word of God in which he finds the fountain of a spiritual experience and to which he turns for confirmation of it. To Calvin the Bible is the Christian law, and the declaration of God's will has authority in its entirety, for belief, church organization, and worship, as well as for ethics. To substitute human reason, which in matters affecting salvation is distorted by original sin, is both impertinent and futile. Here, then, we see a worship based thoroughly on the Bible. The very words of the prayer of confession in Calvin's rite are a conflation of scriptural passages, and the lengthy readings from the Old and New Testaments, and the exposition of God's Word are the tokens of his

---

[2] Adam Mitchell Hunter, *The Teaching of Calvin* (2 ed.; London: James Clarke & Co., 1950).

revelation. The pedagogical aim, to edify the faithful, is as prominent as the desire to give God the glory which an undeviating obedience alone can offer. If, as R. Will holds,[3] there are three major types of worship—the Mystery, the Sacrifice, and the Oracle—then this type of service belongs to the third category, for this worship is a listening to and responding to the Word of God.

Since the biblical criterion in worship is dominant, it is not surprising to find an iconoclastic element present in such worship. If tradition has corrupted the worship which God desires as demanded in his Word, then for all its beauty and dignity, it must go. Hence there comes what those accustomed to a liturgical type of worship would call a bleakness and bareness of ceremonial and furnishings in the Calvinist cultus. Hence, too, there comes an exclusive dependence upon the ear-gate, to the neglect of eye-gate, in worship. With all this limitation, there is also an austere beauty of holiness in this worship, which has created in the Huguenots and the Covenanters a heroic devotion to the living God. Such worship has a strong intellectual and ethical appeal, even if its aesthetic allure is negligible, so that, as a Presbyterian historian of worship has written, "the dread of superstition became itself a superstition in Reformed circles." [4] Such skeletal beauty as this rite possesses is that of an etching, not of a painting. If it is devoid of temptations to aesthetic escapism, it is also liberated from any tendency toward the lushness of sentimentality. It has an objectivity, a sincerity, and a simplicity dependent upon its obeisance to the transcendent God revealed as Judge and Saviour.

[3] *Le Culte* (3 vols.; Paris: Librairie Istra., 1923-35).
[4] Hislop, *op. cit.*, p. 189.

It is not without symbolism, since both baptism and the Lord's Supper re-enact the drama of the gospel itself, as death to sin and resurrection in righteousness. In baptism the washing away of the taint of sin is symbolized (though an affusion hardly stresses this in the present mode of infant baptism), and in the Lord's Supper the death of Christ requiring the death of our egotism is symbolized in the manual acts of breaking the bread and pouring out the wine, which are so clearly emphasized in the modern Presbyterian rite. In this laudable desire to avoid any vain show, however, it is with great difficulty that modern Presbyterian experts in worship are able to persuade ministers and congregations to introduce symbolism and that evocation of the drama of our redemption which finds its climax and its justification in the Incarnation.

In present-day American Presbyterianism there is, however, a desire to combine with free prayers, a definite structure of essential elements in the service and to give the Lord's Supper a more important place in worship, which was undoubtedly Calvin's wish. He recorded for posterity that he wished to introduce a combined service of the Word and of the Lord's Supper each Sunday in Geneva, and was prevented from doing so only by the obduracy of the Genevese. In the Preface to *The Book of Common Worship* of the Presbyterian Church in the U.S.A., the editors write: "Our Presbyterian Church has always emphasized its liberty and has left its ministers free as to the form and order of worship. This freedom, however, has often resulted in worship as formal and as fixed as a prepared liturgy." The aim of the directory is to provide ministers with "treasures in thought and expression that are the inheritance of the Church" and to "encourage Christian congregations to more active participation in Christian worship, which was the custom in the Early Church and is the heritage of the Protestant Reformation."

This Book of Common Worship provides five alternative orders for Sunday Morning Worship. Its structure allows for two groups of prayers that provide for the leading aspects of public devotion. The first is a trio of prayers of Adoration, Confession, and Assurance of Pardon. The second is a quintet of prayers, either preceding or immediately succeeding the Sermon, consisting of prayers of Thanksgiving, Supplication, Intercession, remembering the Communion of Saints, and concluding with the Lord's Prayer. Interspersed are singings of a psalm, two or three hymns (an anthem may be substituted for one hymn), and the large theological or pedagogical elements, comprising: two scripture lessons, the Creed, and the sermon. The congregation's response is found in the praises and offertory.

The Order for the Sacrament of the Lord's Supper or Holy Communion bears comparison with that of the American Prayer Book, which it resembles, so rich is it in historical elements of the Eucharist and so comprehensive. While it is not imposed on all ministers, it is greatly to be hoped that it is regarded as a pattern, so admirable is it. Moreover, although it is clearly dependent upon the Anglican rite, it wisely requires the reading of the Words of Institution as a warrant, not as a prayer, and this enables the celebrant to perform the manual acts of fraction and affusion in obedience to him who said, "Do this in remembrance of me," and thus to dramatize the gospel in action.

Methodist Worship

If Episcopal worship is a combination of Reformed and Roman concepts, Methodist worship in America is a combination of the Anglican tradition, the Puritan emphasis on free prayer, and the effect of the environment of an expanding frontier which made evangelism and simple services the prime need of the times.[5]

The only liturgical or prescribed order which remains in regular Methodist services in America is the Order for The Lord's Supper as celebrated by the Methodist Church.[6] This was the legacy of John Wesley, subsequently modified in part by the example of the American Prayer Book. Wesley's recension of the Anglican Prayer Book was called *The Sunday Service for the Methodists of North America, with Other Occasional Services* and was published in London in 1784. Wesley claimed that this was "a Liturgy little differing from that of the Church of England . . . which I advise all the traveling preachers to use on the Lord's Day in all the congregations." [7] Wesley's changes in the *Book of Common Prayer* consisted of eliminating most of the holy days, the abbreviation of the Lord's Day service, and the omission of several psalms or portions of psalms as "highly improper for the mouths of a Christian congregation." As it happened, the traveling preachers were not disposed to accept Wesley's liturgy for long, partly because they disapproved of the highhanded way in which he had sent out his emissary Dr. Coke to ordain that American by adoption, Asbury, without the permission of the American brethren, partly because they were more familiar with extemporary prayers. Moreover, liberty (as opposed to prescription) was the watchword of

[5] See *The Book of Worship for Church and Home* (New York and Nashville: The Methodist Publishing House, 1944 and later imprints).
[6] See Nolan B. Harmon, *The Rites and Ritual of Episcopal Methodism* (Nashville: Publishing House of the M. E. Church, South, 1926).
[7] Wesley's "Circular Letter" dated at Bristol, Sept. 10, 1784.

the stirring days of the American Revolution. However, the powerful General Conference in North America, did, in its substitution of a Discipline for a Liturgy, retain the Forms for administering the Sacraments and the Occasional Offices, and the Collection of Psalms and Hymns. It was thus that the Anglican heritage, considerably diminished and modified, lived on. As Harmon notes, "It was thus a peculiar twist of fate that Methodism *threw away* the Sunday Service, and *kept* the 'Occasional services.' " [8] Although these forms have never been imposed upon American Methodist ministers, yet they are almost invariably used.

The likeness to the American Prayer Book Order for Holy Communion can be seen in the Methodist Church's Order for the Lord's Supper. Beginning with the communion service proper, the following is an analysis from Harmon's *Understanding The Methodist Church:*

Offering for the Needy
The Offertory Sentences
The Invitation
The General Confession
The Absolution
The Comfortable Words
The Sursum Corda
Trisagion
The Prayer of Humble Access
The Prayer of Consecration
Communication of the Minister
The Communication of the People
The Prayer of Thanksgiving

[8] *Op. cit.,* p. 49.

The Gloria in Excelsis
The Benediction[9]

The substantial difference from Anglican worship is seen in the regular non-Communion services on Sundays. Here the worship has closer links with the Puritan criticisms of the *Book of Common Prayer,* to which, indeed, Wesley had succumbed in part in his revision. This service allows, indeed encourages, the use of free prayers, though this does not in the least prevent a minister from reading his own selection of prayers. There is, however, a real sense that "where the Spirit of the Lord is, there is liberty." Equally dominant is the right of the people to sing the praises of God, which Methodists usually do with unrestrained vigor and gusto. They have never failed to avail themselves of their rich treasury of hymns, breathing a virile practical theology, which Charles Wesley left them, and to which they have added through the years. It would be expected that a denomination which has been aggressive in its evangelistic impact, in which itinerating ministers co-operated with lay local preachers, and for which the saddlebags of the traveling preacher are a rich emotive and historic symbol, would value highly the proclamation of the gospel. Even today the Methodist minister is known primarily as a preacher. Here, too, the Puritan tradition in worship is strong, mollified perhaps by the warmth of pietism. Scriptural holiness was the chief aim of the classical Methodist preachers; this may be endangered occasionally today by a reduction of Christian doctrine to pragmatism, or of Christian thought to "emotional fireworks."

In Methodist worship the note of experienced joy is a

[9] (New York and Nashville: Abingdon Press, 1955), pp. 143-47.

strong one, as also is the devotion of the awakened heart on fire with the love of God. The simplicity and sincerity of the worship is never in doubt, and the call for the moral demands of the Christian life as individual and social service is rarely missing. The danger is that worship may tend to be regarded as merely a preliminary to the preaching, whereas the opposite danger has to be guarded against in Episcopal worship, the possible denigration of preaching. Another potential weakness is that the well-developed sense of fellowship in world-wide Methodism may evoke a complacency which forgets that there is a world-wide community of Christians, and that even this is only a fragment of the greater Church triumphant in heaven. If a historic liturgy runs the risk in its traditional richness of apparent irrelevance, a pragmatic type of service in its contemporary relevance hazards a forgetfulness of the rich heritage of tradition in doctrine and devotion. The Methodist Church of the United States has an insurance against this risk in the historic structure and contents of its Communion Office, but if this is celebrated infrequently and attended by only a proportion of the membership, the risk is not entirely covered. It is certain, however, that the Methodist service has a refreshing simplicity and sincerity, an enviable social warmth, and a zeal for evangelistic outreach.

CHAPTER 8

Baptist, Congregational, and Quaker Worship

THE FIRST TWO OF THESE FORMS OF WORSHIP DEVELOPED out of the Puritan protest against the *Book of Common Prayer* in England in the early seventeenth century; and, while their services bear considerable resemblance to Calvinistic worship, yet they carried Calvin's doctrine of the "inner testimony of the Holy Spirit" in scripture to more radical lengths than Calvin intended. They took the biblical warrant for worship to the point where they were prepared to rely no longer on fixed forms but upon the direct leading of the Holy Spirit in free or extemporaneous prayer. The final step in this movement led to the immanental, immediate, Spirit-inspired worship of the Society of Friends, which saw the light (the *inner* light) in the political convulsions of Commonwealth England.

The English Puritans received their nickname because they wished to reform English Prayer Book worship according to the "pure" Word of God. They included Presbyterians, some evangelical Anglicans, and as their chief protagonists, the Congregationalists and Baptists. On the negative side, they objected to Anglican vestments —the cope and the alb and the surplice were for them "rags of Popery" or "badges of anti-Christ." In their place they proposed to substitute the black Genevan gown and white bands, as a grave (if not funereal) garb for the minister of the Word of God. They further took exception to three "noxious ceremonies" in the Prayer Book: kneeling for the reception of the sacred elements in Holy Communion, as countenancing the Roman miracle of the Mass; the signing of the cross in baptism; and the use of the ring in marriage. It was urged that there was no warrant in scripture for the two latter practices. While the unhappy posture of crouching or lounging persists in many non-episcopal communions for the reception of the elements in the Lord's Supper, the heirs of the Puritans feel no scruple in using the ring in marriage, and some even wish to introduce the signation in baptism, as a token that the child will, God helping him, fight manfully under Christ's banner all his days.

The Puritans [1] criticized the Prayer Book because Anglicans were satisfied with brief, precomposed homilies, instead of sermons that declared the will of God with theological zeal and prophetic fire. They objected to the short lections, which they contemptuously termed "pistling" and "gospelling." They preferred that a complete chapter of the Old and New Testaments should be read at service. They were equally critical of the prayers. Responsive prayers were denounced as "vain repetitions" or "tennis-playing" and they cited I Cor. 14:16 as proof that in the apostolic Church the minister alone led the prayers, the part of the congregation being confined to the concluding "Amen." Indeed, many of them, forgetting that there had been a set liturgy in Geneva, entirely disapproved of forms of prayer. They believed that the minister must pray "in the Spirit" as moved thereto by the Holy Spirit. Their warrant for extemporaneous prayer was Rom. 8:26: "The Spirit also helpeth our infirmity: for we know not how to pray as we ought."

---

[1] For a detailed study of their constructive criticisms see Horton Davies, *The Worship of the English Puritans* (Westminster, Eng.: The Dacre Press, 1948).

They had also serious criticisms to offer of the two gospel sacraments of baptism and the Lord's Supper. In baptism they objected to crossing, to private celebrations —since God keeps his promises in the covenanted community of Christians; and they scrupled godparents, believing that this was a denial of the responsibility of parents, who should answer for the child's growth in grace. The Prayer Book Order for Holy Communion was criticized for its insistence on separate participation in what is intended to be a common meal. They saw no reason for substituting for the original words of delivery, other and unscriptural phrases. They also deprecated the lack of any examination into the lives of intending communicants, believing that unworthy participation in this sacrament endangered the spiritual life of the church member and cheapened the means of grace.

These criticisms, carried over from England and Scotland to North America by immigrants, have accounted for the dislike until recent times of precomposed forms of prayer and an ornate liturgy, among the heirs of the Puritans, the Independents, whether of the Baptist or Congregational persuasions, not forgetting that the Disciples of Christ [2] and many Presbyterians, and not a few Methodists, share some of their views in worship.

But this conception of worship is not a merely negative, dissenting, or niggardly view of worship. It must be recognized that these churches have made several positive contributions to worship. The most notable of them is the use of extempory prayer. Freed from what may prove to be limitations of a liturgy, such prayers can be admirably

[2] The Disciples of Christ practice believer's baptism and celebrate the Lord's Supper every Sunday.

67

adapted to the needs of a congregation. Indeed, as a liturgy presupposes the background of a national or international church, free prayer presupposes the context of a "gathered church," a closely-knit community of men and women covenanting together in holiness. Such free prayers, under the guidance of a devout and beloved minister who knows well both his Bible and his people, have a moving immediacy and relevance that set prayers rarely attain. As Isaac Watts, a Congregational expert in the art of worship and hymn writing, said, "Generals [generalizations] are cold and do not affect us." [3] The same author advised ministers to prepare carefully in private before venturing into the pulpit. Admittedly this lays a heavy duty upon the minister, but if his prayer life has been nurtured on the Scriptures and on the great devotional classics, no complaint need be made. If the prayers are not prepared, or are employed as occasions for rhetoric; if they are a mere farrago of clichés and circumlocutions, or repetitive and unduly long, they are much inferior to reading a liturgy. On the other hand, the ideal is that each service should be a Pentecost, and as Henry Barrowe expressed it, "a confident demanding which faith maketh through the Holy Ghost according to the will of God for the present wants and estates of their hearts or church . . . a pouring forth of the heart unto the Lord."

The Baptists and Congregationalists have a high conception of the proclamation of the Word. Possibly the Presbyterians and the Congregationalists have stressed the ideal of a learned ministry and an educated flock, while the Methodists and the Baptists have concentrated on warm and practical preaching and "striking for" evan-

---

[3] *Works* (ed. Russell), IV, 127.

gelical decisions. While there are many notable exceptions to this generalization, there will be few dissentients to the view that all these communions have stressed the central significance of preaching. This preaching aims at instructing the ignorant, rebuking the errant (even when in high places), comforting the despondent, and building up the faith of the congregation in the gospel. This emphasis has brought with it a corresponding defect: that their services tend to be overly instructional and pedagogical, and insufficiently meditative and mystical.

In the third place, these denominations have stressed (as the Methodists) the rights of the common people to express their ardor in hymns instead of leaving the professional choir to act as their substitutes and proxies in praises. What a deprivation of hymnlore [4] it would be if the Wesleys, Watts, Doddridge, and Bunyan (to take the pre-eminent examples) had never penned a line! It should also be recalled that it is in their hymns that these Christians declare their theological convictions. They do not say, they sing their evangelical creeds. It could also be shown that one of the most significant contributions made by Congregationalists and Baptists to worship was in their preference for a covenant, rather than a creed. They preferred to state their faith as an engagement of the heart, rather than in a series of intellectual propositions.

The distinctive contribution of the Baptists to worship is in their own understanding and expression of baptism as a rite for believers. Theirs is an acted parable of the Christian's burial with Christ and resurrection with him in newness of life, a vivid reminder that the Christian life is a

[4] See Erik Routley's stimulating books, especially *Hymns and Human Life* (New York: Philosophical Library, Inc., 1953) and *I'll Praise My Maker* (London: Independent Press, 1951).

translation from the kingdom of darkness into the kingdom of light.

While Baptists and Congregationalists remain firm in the heritage of the Puritan tradition, there are some among each communion, indeed many among the American Congregationalists,[5] who question the iconoclasm and rejections of the seventeenth century. Their participation in the ecumenical movement has caused them to reconsider the former bleakness of their services, and their tendency to depreciate the traditions of the early and medieval Church and particularly to denigrate the sacrament in favor of the sermon. Beauty is returning, with symbolism, to the house of God. Responses are heard once more in worship.

Quaker Worship

The worship of the Society of Friends goes farther than that of Baptists and Congregationalists in stressing a spiritual worship, which is the result of a quiet and confident waiting upon the Holy Spirit. The pioneer in classical Quaker worship was George Fox (1624-1691), who became increasingly dissatisfied with the formalism, as it seemed to him, of the worship and religion of other bodies of Christian believers in seventeenth-century England. For him worship did not depend upon set places or times or ordained persons or sacraments or even books. He believed that the Spirit of God which gave forth the Scriptures was still at work in the human heart. Worship consisted simply in waiting on the Lord and hearing what he would say. Quaker worship was, therefore, designed to

[5] For evidence of a revaluation see *A Book of Worship for Free Churches,* an admirable compilation by the Congregational Christian official Seminar on worship.

substitute the spirit for the form of worship, by the omission of forms established in advance of the time of meeting. The mode that the revelation would take was essentially unpredictable. As that favorite Quaker text declared: "The wind blows where it wills, and you hear the sound of it, but you do not know whence it comes or whither it goes; so it is with every one who is born of the Spirit" (John 3:8 R.S.V.). The same Spirit was the bond of reconciliation and the impetus to charity for which the Society of Friends is justly admired.

It is, of course, commonplace to state that the Quakers reject the sacraments. It is equally important to insist that they affirm the experience of which the sacraments are believed to be the channels. They believe that no external rite can guarantee sincerity, that in a sacramental universe there should be no limitation of the number of sacraments, and that the requirement of a special ecclesiastical order competent to celebrate sacraments is a denial of the Reformation principle of the priesthood of all believers.[6]

It is easier to criticize than to comprehend the undramatic and immaterial nature of Quaker worship, which has affinities both with the pneumatic worship of the early Church and the silence of Carthusian and Trappist monks.[7] It is a correlate of the doctrine of "Inner Light" —the belief that "the light which lighteth every man coming into the world" will become manifest to the minds and consciences of the waiting disciples. Here is a worship based upon the immanence of God. In the Reformed type of worship the revelation of God is believed to consist in

[6] See Howard Brinton's *Friends for 300 Years* (New York: Harper & Bros., 1952), ch. iv.

[7] See L. Violet Hodgkin, *Silent Worship: The Way of Wonder* (London: Swarthmore Press, 1919).

the objective acts of God in history declared anew and re-experienced in the services; in the worship of the Society of Friends, however, revelation is an inner experience which lights up external events.

The nature of their worship is officially described by the Committee on Christian Relationships of the Religious Society of Friends in Great Britain thus:

Meeting for worship from Sunday to Sunday, and frequently on other days too, Friends have regularly spent a considerable part of their time together in silence, but have always felt free also to minister to one another in the spoken word of exhortation and in uttered prayer, under what they have felt to be the constraining and restraining influence of the Holy Spirit. It is misleading to say that Quaker meetings are silent; their true basis is attentive and expectant waiting on God in worship with full opportunity for ministry. Nor is the silence to be regarded as a rite. In the early days of Friends, Robert Barclay wrote: "True worship consists neither in words nor in silence, as silence, but in a humble dependence of the mind upon God." [8]

A vivid and sympathetic appreciation of a modern American Quaker meeting is contained in Christopher Isherwood's novel *The World in the Evening:*

Nevertheless, the Silence, in its odd way, was coming to life. Was steadily filling up the bare white room, like water rising in a tank. Every one of us contributed to it, simply by being present. Togetherness grew and tightly enclosed us until it seemed that we must all be breathing in unison and keeping time with our heart-beats. It was massively alive and somehow,

[8] *Ways of Worship*, eds. Pehr Edwall, Eric Hayman, and William D. Maxwell (New York: Harper & Bros., 1951), an ecumenical account of worship in the modern world. Used by permission.

unimaginably ancient, like the togetherness of Man in the primeval caves.[9]

The novelist's account captures the stillness, the expectancy, the unity (Fox speaks of "the hidden unity of the Divine Being"), the simplicity, the integrity, and the spontaneity of Quaker worship.

This concept of a "constraining and restraining" Spirit in communion with the expectant group in silence or in economy of speech is profoundly relevant in our ear-splitting world where we "have no time to stand and stare." It is the essential Quaker contribution to the world Church, for it shows that the highest worship is adoration —speechless humility before the sheer magnificent generosity of God. Its purity and simplicity is a salutary reminder that worship can be made too artificial by excessive ceremonial and ritualistic exactitude, and that even a revelation may become fossilized as an external law.

On the other hand, the austere ardors of Quakerism have never appealed to the many. Thomas Hodgkin, himself a Quaker, admits this, in saying:

It is not equally adapted to all mental conditions; it needs to be introduced with discretion, it will not compensate for the neglect of the gift of teaching; it is a rule more fitted for those who have made some advance in the Christian life, than for those who are still on the threshold.[10]

Quakerism appeals to the spirit of man—to man, in other words, as a disembodied spirit, or to man as introvert. What of the aesthetic side of his nature, or his activism? Finally, the sense of the immanence of God, his nearness, must be balanced by the sense of his transcendence, his otherness.

[9] New York: Random House, Inc., 1954.
[10] *The Fellowship of Silence*, p. 87.

II
THE CONTENT OF WORSHIP

—————•••—————

CHAPTER 9

Preparation for Worship:
Private Prayer

IN CHRISTIAN WORSHIP THERE ARE TWO MOVEMENTS: GOD'S
approach to us, and our approach to God. God's approach
is by revelation through scripture lessons and sacrament,
which declare the mighty acts of God for us, and in the
sermon, which expounds them. The other side of worship
is our response to God's revelation. This is made in praise
and, supremely, in prayer. "To have a God," said Luther,
"is to pray to Him."

The reader may wonder what place, if any, private
prayer has in a service of corporate worship. The answer
is, that apart from preparation by way of private prayer
and meditation for each service God cannot reveal himself
to the worshipers, nor can they in turn make a true dedication of themselves in worship. True worship involves on
man's part a receptive heart and a surrendered will. Thus
worship becomes more real through preparation by means
of regular private prayers in the home and before the commencement of the service.

For prayer to be the intimate conversation between God
and the worshiper, which it is intended to be, all doubts
and difficulties that hamper prayer must be removed. The

74

praying man must "ask in faith, nothing wavering." As to the causes of "wavering," the usual intellectual difficulties are fivefold:

1. It is often thought that prayer is a form of self-deception. The beginner in prayer may think of this activity much as the little girl who, watching a man telephoning from a phone booth, remarked excitedly to her mother, "Mummy, look—there's a man talking to himself." Prayer is not a method of reminding ourselves of our Christian duties. It is a real approach to God the Father. It is enough for the Christian to remember that our Lord could not dispense with prayer.

2. A second objection sometimes urged against prayer is that since God knows everything, it is unnecessary to pray to him. Indeed, it has been suggested that it is presumptuous to trouble God with human worries. The important fact is not that God is omniscient, but that he is graciously willing to listen to us and help us. It is crude to think of God as if he were a disinterested manager of the universe who will not condescend to notice mortal office boys. Our Lord made it convincingly clear that God is interested in his children. The fact of the Cross is itself certain proof of his overwhelming concern for humanity.

3. Prayer, it is objected, is the coward's castle, the refuge of the disappointed and the discouraged. It is, of course, true that men naturally turn to their Maker when in difficulties. "All lost! to prayers, to prayers!" cry the shipwrecked mariners in *The Tempest*. But that in itself is a sign of man's dependence upon God. It is a recognition that there are situations beyond human help. The answer to this difficulty can also be found in the teaching and practice of Christ. In the garden of Gethsemane, when the shadow of the imminent cross lay over his prostrate figure,

75

Jesus cried in an agony of sweat, "Father, . . . let this cup pass away from me." If our Lord needed such supernatural strength, surely his servants do.

4. Another criticism urges that prayer is favoritism, a human attempt to make a convenience out of God. It is reminiscent of the small girl who prayed each night, "Please God, send me a tricycle for Christmas"; then, when Christmas came and the desired gift did not materialize, she stopped praying. When asked by her parents why she had stopped praying, she answered, "I've finished with God now." If prayer is only a statement of our requests, it is defective prayer. That is why Christians ought only to ask God for what they think would help them to fulfill his will. For that reason our Lord ended his Gethsemane prayer, "Not my will, but thine, be done." The Lord's Prayer, the perfect pattern of all prayers, has as its first requests, "Hallowed be thy name. Thy kingdom come. Thy will be done." These preface the personal requests, "Give us this day our daily bread." Favoritism can be obviated by including personal requests in that setting.

5. The fifth criticism maintains that modern science has exploded any possibility of prayers being answered. We live, say the scientists, in a universe of rigid laws. If God made it thus, why expect him to break laws of his own devising? This question can be parried by replying, "Is God to be ruled by his own laws?" It could also be stated, with accuracy, that modern scientists are not so prone nowadays to dogmatize about the rigidity of the laws of the universe. A modern scientific principle is known as the "Principle of Indeterminacy." That means, quite simply, that the course of a particular atom cannot be exactly predicted. Eddington sums up the position: "Thus far we have shown that modern physics is drifting away from the

postulate that the future is predetermined, ignoring it rather than deliberately rejecting it." [1] The Christian is therefore not urged to believe that the universe is a prisoner of rigid laws. Moreover, since he is a believer in the Incarnation and the Resurrection, he should be the last to deny either the intervention of God or his ability to answer prayers.

Prayer is the exercise of faith. It is also the oxygen of the spiritual life. But it must be practiced regularly and thoughtfully. Just as an acquaintance becomes a friend through the agency of many meetings and conversations, so regular prayer deepens intimacy with God and trust in him. But even if the necessary faith in prayer is present, as also the wish to devote a regular part of each day to its exercise, practical obstructions may make it difficult to fulfill the resolve to pray. It may be objected that it is hard to find the necessary time in a crowded day. If, however, the Christian is too busy for prayer, it can only be urged in reply that he is *too* busy!

The most suitable times are early in the morning or late at night. It is wise to begin the day with a few minutes spent in prayer and meditation. Those five minutes provide time enough in which to thank God for all his benefits and to resolve that day, with divine help, to carry out some work for him. It is also beneficial for the culture of the spiritual life, to set aside time for prayer when the day is over. In such a period, time could be found for remembering before God persons and causes of great concern to us, such as the church of Christ and our friends. Furthermore, a deeper reality would be brought into confession, if the person praying were to recollect where he had failed

---

[1] A. S. Eddington, *The Nature of the Physical World* (London: Cambridge University Press, 1932), p. 307.

God during the day and if he had fulfilled the morning's resolutions to work for God. Prayer need not be lengthy; and it need not be couched in scriptural language, as long as it is thoughtful and sincere.

Supposing that time can be set aside for prayer, it may be difficult to find a quiet place in a crowded household. But there is one place where prayer can usually be offered in perfect solitude, and that is a bedroom. And the best attitude for prayer is kneeling beside the bed. It is the right attitude because it expresses humility. People kneel as a sign of respect to royalty; surely we should kneel in the presence of the King of kings!

Another and serious practical difficulty is lack of concentration. Wandering thoughts take the mind away from God, with the result that there is much repetition and discouragement. It is always wise to concentrate in silence on what God has done, before speaking to him. If Christ fills the thoughts of the Christian, such a person will easily exclude the world in his prayers. It is possible to do this simply by thinking of our Lord, his words and works, his birth, his temptations, his life, his death, his resurrection, and their meaning for the Christian life. This, of itself, would constitute a silent prayer of thanksgiving for the love of God shown in Christ. If it is still found to be difficult to concentrate, then the following practical suggestions may be of some assistance.

To avoid a distracted mind it is wise to read over a short portion of scripture, perhaps a Psalm, before beginning to pray. Occasionally it is helpful to read some incident in the life of Christ or of the apostles, and to pray to God for the qualities of soul exhibited in the incident. Prayers can be given variety and reality by keeping a notebook in which are written the names of friends and causes which should be remembered in prayer. Another wise rule is to avoid spending all the time in praying *against* a temptation. It is better to meditate on the strength of Christ and on the overcoming of the temptation.

Prayer requires practice. The best advice on the exercise of the gift of prayer is found in the New Testament. Much of it could be learned by careful meditation on the following passages. The way of prayer is shown in Luke 11:1-4; 18:1-14; Mark 11:25, and Heb. 11:6. The ensuing passages teach the need of simplicity and sincerity in prayer: Matt. 6:5-8; 11:25-30; and Mark 11:22-26. Proof is offered that prayers are heard in Isa. 55:6-11; Ps. 20; John 16:23-28; and Acts 2:1-4. The following passages show prayer as service to God: Isa. 58:6-8; Matt. 10:40-42; 25:31-40; and Luke 10:25-27.

In conclusion, only those who come to corporate worship as praying Christians are able to offer God acceptable homage. Such will participate actively in the service, listening eagerly to the Word of God, in lesson and sermon, as their marching orders; and through the prayers they will be meeting again in spirit with the God whom they have learned to know and love in private. Preparation for worship by private prayer and meditation makes the approach to God richer as a sincere tribute of thanksgiving; and the receptive heart will carry most away from a service.

CHAPTER 10

Common Prayers

THE PURPOSE AND THE RANGE OF COMMON PRAYERS ARE
excellently expressed in the Exhortation contained in the
Prayer Book as proposed in 1928:

> Beloved, we are come together in the presence of Almighty
> God and of the whole company of heaven to offer unto Him
> through our Lord Jesus Christ our worship and praise and
> thanksgiving; to make confession of our sins; to pray, as well
> for others as for ourselves, that we may know more truly the
> greatness of God's love and shew forth in our lives the fruits
> of His grace; and to ask on behalf of all men such things as
> their well-being doth require. Wherefore let us kneel in silence,
> and remember God's presence with us now.

If this exhortation is analyzed, it will be seen that there
are five main branches of Christian prayer. If a service is
to be complete it must include each one of them.

The first type of prayer is *Thanksgiving*. We come "to
offer . . . through our Lord Jesus Christ our worship and
praise and thanksgiving." True worship is "a sacrifice of
praise" (Heb. 13:15).

The second mood of prayer is inevitably *Confession*. As
the Christian contemplates the perfections of God, his
holiness, love, constancy, and the infinite cost of our redemption to God, he is forced to realize with shame the
poverty of his own spiritual life. He is, by contrast with
God, impure, callous, fickle, and insulting. In the words

of the General Confession, "there is no health in us." The vision of God drives us to our knees in confession.

The third part of prayer naturally beseeches God to enable us to be what we ought to be. It is *Petition*. We humbly ask for forgiveness. If the thanksgiving is the Christian saying, "Thank you," and the confession is the "Sorry," then the petition is the Christian's "Please." We ask God for the graces of the Christian life.

But we do not pray only for ourselves. We come "to pray, *as well for others* as for ourselves." Remembering that God is our heavenly Father, we hold up before him the needs of our brothers in the world. There is no limit to the range of intercession. We may rightly expect, however, that intercession will bear in mind the following needs: the universal Church, God's agency for the fulfilling of his purpose in the world; our own country: its leaders in government and its citizens; and all who are in great need, such as the sick and dying, the unemployed and poor, the disabled and the bereaved. Such pleading before God will be an effective reminder to us of our Christian duty to "bear one another's burdens, and so fulfil the law of Christ." But that is not its main purpose. The meaning of intercession is to make available all the powerful resources of God for those in need. While prayer is no substitute for practical sympathy, it is in itself a means of help. "The . . . prayer of a righteous man availeth much," says James. (5:16 K.J.V.)

The fifth part of prayer is *Dedication*. Its aim is that we may "show forth in our lives the fruits of His grace." To offer such a prayer in all sincerity is the greatest single contribution we make to Christian worship. It is fitting that dedication should be stressed late in the service. This

81

ensures that worship is not an escape from life by reminding us of our duty in the world outside the Church.

Having examined the moods or parts of prayer, we now turn to look at the forms of prayer. There are three main forms, represented by three traditions of worship:

1. First we have liturgical prayer, which is characteristic of the worship of Orthodox, Roman, Lutheran, and Anglican Christians. What are its advantages? Chief among them are the following: the use of set prayers enables the congregation to take a vocal part in the prayers; the uniformity of a liturgy means that there is an impressive unity among all the churches which are using the same prayer book at the same time; set prayers make available the rich treasure of the devotions of the saints in all ages in dignified and beautiful language.

2. But even the finest prayer books are open to certain criticisms. It is the realization of their weaknesses that accounts for the stressing of the importance of free or extemporary prayers in the Free Churches. The pioneers in this tradition felt that the repetition of the same prayers, year in and year out, made for formality and even insincerity. "Familiarity breeds contempt" or, at least, indifference. Moreover, common prayer can deal only with the common needs of our humanity. For that reason it is likely to be impersonal. There is no provision in it for special local needs or occasions. For these reasons the Free Churches prefer the extemporary prayers of their ministers, who pray as the Holy Spirit moves them. Their sanction for this practice is found in Rom. 8:26: "In like manner the Spirit also helpeth our infirmity: for we know not how to pray as we ought; but the Spirit himself maketh intercession for us." Such prayers are spontaneous and personal, an overheard conversation with God. But it is not

to be supposed that they are faultless. Isaac Watts had to counsel the ministers of his day to prepare their prayers and not to trust to "sudden motions." Unprepared free prayer may be undisciplined "rambling round the Universe"; it may be spoiled by unsuitable expressions; it may involve too much repetition. At its best, however, it is a moving and exalting experience.

3. The third kind of prayer is that developed by the Quakers, or the Society of Friends. It is silent prayer. This also depends not upon prayer books, but upon the moving of the Holy Spirit in the hearts of the congregation. This type of prayer requires a profound training in the culture of the spiritual life. It involves meditation and an ability to retire from the concerns and anxieties of the outer world. It is not suitable for the beginner or for those who in corporate worship require vocal expression of prayer for the assembled worshipers. To most people it would seem to be a technique more suitable for private devotions than for public worship.

However, it has served as a protest against "vain repetitions" in worship, and many devout lives have been nourished by it. It is dangerous to follow this technique at the commencement of the spiritual life, as the ensuing story makes plain. A small boy had heard his minister extol the importance of listening to God in prayer in silence. He put this into operation for several weeks. His parents noticed that when his vocal prayer had ended there was a long interval before he said, "Amen." Then one day he reverted to his usual custom of a hurried "Amen" at the end of his vocal prayer. The parents asked him why he did this. He said, "I listened to what God had to say, but I got tired of hearing him say, 'Don't forget to brush your teeth.' " Obviously, the child was too immature to concentrate on the thought of God in the silence.

Hitherto the three traditions have followed their own techniques in splendid isolation. Now there is no reason why a service should not include a liturgical portion in which minister and people could join together vocally, an extemporary prayer or prayers in which the minister could be more personally relevant, and a period of silence for meditation and dedication. Each type of technique has justified itself by producing the fruits of the Christian life. In a reunited Church all will be needed.

In conclusion, we shall identify and examine three well-known types of prayer.

1. The *Collect*. This is easily identified as a brief petition which almost invariably concludes with "through Jesus Christ our Lord." A famous example from the *Book of Common Prayer* proceeds:

Almighty God, unto whom all hearts be open, all desires known, and from whom no secrets are hid; Cleanse the thoughts of our hearts by the inspiration of Thy Holy Spirit, that we may perfectly love thee, and worthily magnify thy holy Name; through Christ our Lord.

The collect opens with an invocation: "Almighty God." It continues with a description of the attributes of God: "unto whom all hearts be open." Then it makes a definite petition, "Cleanse the thoughts of our hearts," following with a reason why this is acceptable to God: "that we may perfectly love thee, and worthily magnify thy holy Name." It concludes, as nearly all collects do, in the name of our Lord. All collects will be seen to have this fivefold structure: (*a*) invocation, (*b*) description, (*c*) petition, (*d*) aim of petition, and (e) conclusion. The advantage of a collect is its brevity and its compression of thought.

2. A longer type of prayer is the *Litany*. This term may be used of any series of prayers which contain responsive parts for the people, such as, "Lord, hear our prayer and let our cry come unto thee." But in the *Book of Common Prayer* it is used more strictly of the General Supplication. Its most frequent response is: "Good Lord, deliver us," or "We beseech thee to hear us, good Lord." It includes both petition and intercession. Its chief merit is that it enables both congregation and minister to take a vocal part in common prayer.

3. The third type of prayer is the *Bidding* prayer. This is not a direct approach to God. It is a series of biddings or orders to the congregation that they shall remember the causes to be enumerated in their own prayers. This form of prayer is effective only if time enough is allowed for the congregation to formulate their own prayers. If it is hurried through and recited as a catalogue, it loses reality.

Ultimately the contents of prayer are more important than the technique or type of prayer. But it will have been seen that each form of prayer—liturgical, free, or silent—has its own important place in Christian worship. Whichever type is used, as long as it is prayed with faith and sincerity, it is valuable.

CHAPTER 11

The Reading and Preaching of God's Word

JACOB IN HIS DIVINE VISION SAW "A LADDER SET UP ON the earth, and the top of it reached to heaven: and behold the angels of God ascending and descending on it" (Gen. 28:12). We might take that as a picture of worship, of communications between God and us. The angels ascending the ladder would represent our messages to God, our prayers, our praises, and our offerings. The angels descending the ladder would represent God's messages to us, the lessons and the sermon.

When the Bible is called the "Word of God," we mean that it contains God's word or message to us. We hear that message in the reading of scripture and in the preaching, based upon scripture. Why is it important that we should hear this old, old story of long ago? It is of the first importance because it is by hearing and understanding it that we become mature Christians. But we must listen in faith. That is, we must not listen to the Bible as, for instance, we might listen to a quiz program on television, or to a bedtime story, or to a political speaker. In a quiz program we listen to various experts giving their opinions; a bedtime story is interesting, but we know that the events didn't really happen; a political speech aims at getting us interested in a certain course of action, and often such speeches exaggerate.

But when listening to the Bible we need to be much more serious. For through the stories in it God is speaking

86

to us, and we cannot dismiss what he says as if it was no concern of ours. Although in fact we are listening to words of long ago, perhaps the words of Isaiah the prophet foretelling the coming of the Messiah or rebuking the Israelites for their rebelliousness, or perhaps the words of the Word of God himself (Jesus Christ) beside the lake of Galilee or on the cross, yet God may be speaking these words to us *personally*. To listen with faith means to listen in obedience: to hear these words as commands, or warnings, or promises to us. It is this kind of serious listening that helps to make us Christians. That is why the lessons and the sermon occupy a central position in the service. We shall think of the sacraments later; it is useful to remember that they dramatize the Word of God, while lessons and sermons proclaim it by word of mouth. The lesson and sermon speak to the ear, the sacraments to the eye in the acts of baptism, and the breaking of the bread and the pouring out of the wine.

What is a sermon? How does it differ from an essay, or a lecture, or a speech? An essay does not have the authority of a sermon; it expresses the personal and often fanciful opinions of the essayist. Take Charles Lamb's "Dissertation upon Roast Pig," for instance. You would not think of taking his suggestion seriously, that the best pork is roasted by being burned in a paper house. He is only indulging his fancy and amusing you by his quaint ideas. Is a sermon, then, like a lecture? Not quite, because the lecturer's main duty is to impart facts interestingly—he is not delivering a message to you.

Is the sermon like a speech? Again, not quite; but a speech aims at getting you to support a particular line of action. The Democratic or Republican candidate for Federal or state political office will paint a glowing picture of his party colleagues in office and an equally depressing one of the scenes of ruin that will ensue if his opponents are elected. He uses arguments, facts, and statistics to appeal to your reason, and imagination to appeal to your emotions —all to get your vote. While a sermon should appeal to both light and heat that your mind and heart may move your will to serve God, it is rarely appropriate to discuss controversial issues in the pulpit. Moreover, a meditative type of sermon might not readily lead to any single type of Christian action but to adoration that might be expressed in a variety of ways.

The Oxford English Dictionary defines a sermon as "Extempore or written discourse from the pulpit by way of religious instruction or exhortation." The last four words are the important part of the definition. A sermon gives information about God's will or exhorts (encourages) men in the name of God. A sermon is the proclamation of the gospel. Its function is to tell the congregation of the mighty acts of God declared in the Bible. It will speak of how God created the world and made man in God's own image; of how, when man rebelled and sinned, God planned human salvation by sending Jesus Christ into the world. It will declare the words, the deeds, and the meaning of this son of Mary who was also Son of God. It will go on to speak of his cross, his resurrection, his ascension, and of his sending of the Holy Spirit to the disciples at Pentecost. It will tell of this world-wide community, the Church, which contains all Christians of every race and tongue. It will, above all, seek to make those who listen long to share the privileges of the gospel. This is the Word of God enshrined in the Scriptures which it is the minister's duty to unfold Sunday by Sunday.

Heinrich Vogel, in his book *The Iron Ration of a Chris-*

tian, says: "A Sermon is the proclamation of that message which comes to us from God Himself." He then goes on to describe what this preaching is:

You remember the story of the messenger who came from the Battle of Marathon. When the Greeks prevailed over the superior power of Persia and so saved their fatherland, a messenger ran all the way to Athens to bring the news of the victory, and then collapsed and died. This messenger had not philosophized about the victory. He did not proceed to offer a few observations on what a victory was and what one must do in order to win one. Nor did he compose a poem of how they had longed for victory. None of that could have saved the Athenians from the Persians. He cried out to them quite simply the fact and the truth: "We have won." . . .

A preacher is a messenger from the King of all kings, proclaiming in His name and by His order the news of victory; not of our victory, but of God's victory, the victory of His grace in Christ crucified and risen for us. A preacher stands in the pulpit or by the coffin, or wherever he may be, not as a poet or a philosopher trying to express his religious ideas and feelings, but as a messenger of God's truth.[1]

Now we must look at the different kinds of sermons. In general, there are three distinct types. The first of these is *expository,* so called because it is a simple exposition or explanation of a passage of scripture. Such a sermon will take an incident or a story or a parable from the Bible and unfold its meaning simply. It will conclude by applying the point of the sermon to the Christian life of the congregation. One of the most famous preachers of this kind of sermon was Campbell Morgan, of Westminster Chapel. The great merit of such sermons is that they do

[1] Tr. W. A. Whitehouse (London: Student Christian Movement Press, 1942), p. 184. Used by permission.

not inflict the preacher's last-minute meditations or his last week's reading on the congregation; rather they concentrate on the timeless truth of the Word of God.

The second type of sermon is the *doctrinal*. This type of sermon instructs the congregation in the articles of Christian belief. A renowned doctrinal preacher of Victorian days was F. W. Robertson of Brighton, whose sermons on Christian doctrine are justly famous. In modern days when the attacks of science and the attraction of other religions have made a restatement of the Christian faith necessary, such sermons are quite commonly heard. They make their appeal to the intellect.

The third type of sermon is *topical*. This heading covers sermons good and bad. In this connection "topical" is occasionally used as a word of abuse to describe a sermon which is smartly up-to-date or makes capital out of recent happenings. There is, however, another kind of sermon properly called "topical" which is to be commended. This type of sermon deals with practical Christianity, applying the lessons of scripture to abuses in our public life. Famous preachers of topical and social sermons, though they often preached doctrinal sermons, were John Wesley, F. D. Maurice, R. W. Dale, Charles Gore, Scott Holland, Silvester Horne, Hensley Henson, Walter Rauschenbusch, and Harry Emerson Fosdick, happily still with us. On them the mantle of the prophets fell. Just as Amos and Hosea denounced the luxury, the avarice, the injustice, and the corruption of their times, so the preachers of the "social gospel" reminded the wealthy of their responsibility for the oppressed and the poor. To take but one instance, it was a topical sermon preached by Hugh Price Hughes from the platform of the West London Mission, demanding Parnell's resignation for immorality, that led to that statesman's removal from the political scene. "We love Ireland," he said, "but our first obedience and our highest devotion must be to God. . . . We stand immovably on this eternal rock; what is morally wrong can never be politically right." [2] That utterance was typical of the strength of topical preaching at its best.

The dangers of this type of sermon have already been pointed out. Too often the preacher sets up as politician and suggests new plans for the improvement of the country. That should be left to the experts in government. On the other hand, if legislation is contemplated or introduced which breaks the laws of God, the preacher would be criminally negligent if he held his peace.

It is as well to have some useful tests by which to estimate whether or not a sermon is a good one. Most people say a sermon is a good one if it is interesting. But that is not a true test, because the preacher may not have given you any message from God, and yet have been very interesting. The first test of a good sermon is to ask: Was this a fair explanation of the text or passage of scripture? Was it good exposition? That is the preacher's main task. Second, is it easy to remember the main parts or headings of the sermon? If the gist of a sermon cannot be remembered, then its message did not get across to you, and it is a poor sermon. Good sermons must leave a lasting impression. Thirdly, was the sermon easy to understand? That is, was the language simple and unacademic; were the illustrations clear, and the thoughts lucid? Last, you should ask: Was the message helpful? If a sermon fulfils these conditions it is a real proclamation of the Word of God.

There is space for only a few lines on scripture lessons.

[2] See the fascinating little book, *The Nonconformist Conscience,* by H. F. Lovell Cocks (London: Independent Press, n.d.) .

If the reader belongs to the Anglican Church, he will use a lectionary, or calendar of lessons—that is, the lessons will be so arranged that in the course of the year the congregation will have heard read to them the finest passages of the Bible. If the reader is a member of a Free Church, it is possible that he also will hear both Old Testament and New Testament lessons at each service. It is, however, more likely that the lessons will illustrate the theme of the sermon. Each method has its advantages and disadvantages. The advantage of a lectionary is that a congregation is not likely to suffer from hearing the same passages read over and over again, as is often the case when the minister makes his own little anthology. A calendar or lectionary ensures that a wide range of the Bible is known by the congregation. The advantage of selecting lessons to illustrate the theme of the sermon is that this gives added point to them and makes the service more of a unity.

The real purpose of both lessons and sermon is, as we have seen, that they shall proclaim God's good news, the gospel. If that is done, and there is a faithful, obedient congregation listening to them, then there is true worship offered to God.

CHAPTER 12

Praise

JOHN MILTON, IN HIS POEM "IL PENSEROSO," HAS DESCRIBED
in classic words the sheer delight and elevation of spirit
that music brings into worship:

> There let the pealing Organ blow,
> To the full voic'd Quire below,
> In Service high, and Anthems cleer,
> As may with sweetness, through mine ear,
> Dissolve me into extasies,
> And bring all Heav'n before mine eyes.

The music of instrument and voice is able to interpret
our emotions perfectly. If we mourn the death of Christ
on the cross and our own sins, where shall we find a more
poignant expression of grief than in Bach's setting to "It
is finished" in the *Saint John Passion?* The plaintive fall-
ing of violins expresses thoughts more deep than tears. If
we wish to express the joy of Christ's resurrection and
reign, where can it be found more triumphantly sung than
in Handel's "Hallelujah Chorus" in *The Messiah;* or, to
take a more familiar expression, in Charles Wesley's hymn
"O for a thousand tongues to sing my great Redeemer's
praise"?

Music not only serves to express our religious emotions;
it also provides a common medium for the corporate expression of praise. Music is a social art, an activity in which
all can join. It is used in Christian worship as the family's
joint act of thanksgiving. As J. O. Dobson writes: "It is a
significant thing that harmony developed in the music of

Christian worship. For harmony is an expression of fellowship in a common intention, a common allegiance variously declared, yet without discord." [1]

Our praise is expressed in three ways: through chants, anthems, and hymns. The oldest is, of course, the *chant* or psalm. The Hebrew Psalter was the first hymnbook of the Christian family. It would be familiar from childhood to our Lord and the disciples as the praise book of the temple. Since those early days the psalms have given tongue to the praises of Christians of all denominations. "Here," writes Evelyn Underhill, "Catholic and Covenanter sing from one service book, and acknowledge themselves to be brothers under their skins." [2] The vast range of experiences contained in the Psalter makes it eminently suitable for the varied expression of praise. There are found national exaltation and national humiliation, praises suitable for national festivals, expressions of the soul baffled by the problem of evil and innocent suffering; and the moods range from prostrate confession to soaring delight and confidence in God.

The psalms are used in the worship of all communions. They are accorded a position of greater honor, perhaps, in Roman and Anglican churches than they receive in Free Churches. This may be because they are more difficult to sing than hymns and, therefore, are most suitably rendered by a trained choir. In churches with a liturgical tradition it is the function of the choir to sing, the congregation often being mute listeners. In the Free Churches where the praise is offered by the whole congregation, chants are less frequently sung. The great advantage of chants is that they sound forth the actual words of the Scriptures.

---

[1] *Worship* (New York: The Macmillan Co., 1941).
[2] *Op. cit.*

If the people could not readily sing chants in the Free Churches, they joined with alacrity in the singing of *metrical psalms*. To this day the metrical psalms are the chief vehicle of praise employed by the Church of Scotland. Because they were rhymed they could be easily memorized by congregations in days when books were scarce and costly. They were popular not only in Scotland, but also in the English Established Church during the sixteenth and seventeenth centuries.

The *anthem* is almost always sung by the choir. It is usually a passage of scripture or a poem or prayer set to complicated music, and therefore suited only to a choir and not for congregational use. Anthems have given musical composers more scope for their creative talents than hymns, and many modern anthems are excellently set. It is not uncommon to find them set to the music of such famous composers as Tchaikovsky, Mozart, Gounod, Mendelssohn, and Bach, not to mention such modern composers as Elgar, Vaughan Williams, and Holst.

The most common and most popular medium of praise is the *hymn*. The oldest hymns go back to the early days of the Church or to the Middle Ages. Among them are the *Te Deum Laudamus,* a fine confession of faith, the *Veni, Creator Spiritus* (translated as "Come, Holy Ghost, our souls inspire"), the *Jesu, dulcis memoria* of Bernard (translated as "Jesu, the very thought of Thee with sweetness fills the breast"), and Thomas Aquinas' great eucharistic hymn translated as "O bread to pilgrims given."

The second great period of hymn writing and hymn singing was the Reformation. Luther spread the new teaching in hymns of his own making in the German language. One of the most famous of these is in every Protestant hymnbook—"A safe stronghold our God is still."

In England the great period of hymn writing was the eighteenth century, associated with the names of Watts, Doddridge, Wesleys, Cowper, and Newton. Through them the people were enabled to play their full part in worship. Perhaps it is only to be expected that the Free Churches should have been the pioneers in introducing the singing of hymns into English worship. For in their church government they had expressed more completely the Reformation and scriptural doctrine of "the priesthood of all believers." In their worship the praise was offered not by a trained choir, but by the whole congregation.

In the Anglican Church, the responses of the liturgy were at one time the people's part in worship; [3] for Free Church congregations the hymns were the equivalent. The importance of hymns in Free Churches can be seen in these quotations from Bernard L. Manning's *The Hymns of Wesley and Watts:*

Hymns are for us Dissenters what the liturgy is for the Anglican. They are the framework, the setting, the conventional, the traditional part of divine service as we use it. They are, to adopt the language of the liturgiologists, the Dissenting Use. . . .

We mark times and seasons, celebrate festivals, . . . and expound doctrines by hymns.[4]

In the latter quotation will be seen the importance of hymns in a Free Church service. No formal creed is recited, but the hymns are themselves expositions of the Christian faith. There are no appropriate collects or epistles to mark the Christian seasons in Free Church worship, but the hymns do that instead. Further, they are the living expression of the Christian's experience of God.

[3] Hymns are, of course, a normal part of Anglican services today.
[4] (London: The Epworth Press, 1942), pp. 133, 135.

CHAPTER 13

The Sacraments: Baptism and the Lord's Supper

WHAT IS A SACRAMENT? THE ANSWER GIVEN IN THE CATE-chism in the *Book of Common Prayer* is: "An outward and visible sign of an inward and spiritual grace given unto us . . . by Christ himself." A sacrament is a dramatic demonstration of the gospel. The actions are the pouring out of water in infant baptism or immersion in believer's baptism, and the breaking of the bread and the pouring out of the wine in the Lord's Supper. The water symbolizes the gift of salvation—the cleansing of forgiveness and the rebirth to new life. The bread and wine symbolize the sacrifice upon Calvary by which we obtain forgiveness of our sins and eternal life.

The two sacraments are, therefore, dramatic re-presentations of the benefits of the gospel. We are now in a position to understand the definition given in the official statements of Congregationalists and Presbyterians in the Savoy Declaration and the Westminster Confession. This runs: "A Sacrament is a holy ordinance instituted by Christ, wherein by sensible [i.e., visible] signs Christ and the new covenant are represented, sealed and applied to believers." Certain actions speak louder than words. For instance, Churchill, when visiting an area shattered by enemy action had only to part his middle and forefinger in a "V" sign to raise the spirits of the bystanders; or, as you enter a sick room a friend warns you to tread softly and make your visit as short as possible simply by placing her finger on her lips. The sacraments in the same way, by "sensible signs," re-enact the message of the gospel and convey its benefits.

1. Baptism

The scriptural authority for baptism is found in the concluding words of Matthew's Gospel (28:19) wherein our Lord commissions his apostles to "make disciples of all the nations, baptizing them into the name of the Father and of the Son and of the Holy Ghost." The Acts of the Apostles records nine separate cases of baptism being administered and proves that the apostles were faithful to their Lord's teaching. It was quite clearly the accepted method by which people were admitted into the membership of the Church, as a sign that they had died to the old life and were reborn to the new way of life in Christ. It follows that as most of the members were adults, the act of baptism was a definite public confession of the lordship of Christ. It cannot be ascertained from the New Testament whether infants were baptized or not. It may be that they were, because, we are told that whole households were baptized (Acts 10:48, Cornelius and his household; 16:15, Lydia and her household; and 16:33, the Philippian jailer and his household).

To this day the Baptist denomination restricts the rite of the baptism to believers, refusing to baptize children. The reasons for this restriction are threefold, as enumerated by Wheeler Robinson.[1] The first reason is the psychological value of the rite for believers. The immersion of adults corresponds more closely than the effusion of water over infants to Paul's description: "We were buried

[1] *The Life and Faith of the Baptists* (Rev. ed.; London: Kingsgate Press, n.d.)

therefore with him through baptism into death: that like as Christ was raised from the dead through the glory of the Father, so we also might walk in newness of life" (Rom. 6:4). Believer's baptism expresses vividly the confession of conversion from darkness to light. It is an impressive reminder to the subject of baptism that he has entered a new way of life. Second, believer's baptism unmistakably emphasizes conversion. It celebrates the decisive step taken by the individual in embracing the Christian faith. This ceremony insists upon an individual experience of God. In the third place, it has a confessional value. Immersion is an acted parable of the Lord's death, burial, and resurrection, and implies on the part of the baptized person a confession of the lordship of Christ. It is an "epitomized Apostles' Creed."

What, then, are the values preserved by infant baptism? (*a*) Infant baptism preserves the thought that God's covenant is made to believers and to their children. The family is a social unity and infant baptism declares that the privileges of protection from evil, and of inspiration which membership in a Christian family includes, belong to the child. (*b*) Infant baptism also stresses the divine initiative in our salvation, as believer's baptism emphasizes the human response. It makes it clear that God does not wait for our repentance; he sends his Son to bring about that repentance. If we love him, it is because he first loved us (I John 4:10, 19). The gospel comes to us not in response to our faith or our good works, but from the will and love of God. Moreover, the fact that our Lord blessed the children (Mark 10:13-16) manifestly declares that his blessing was not confined to those who came to him in conscious faith or penitence. The words "For of such is the kingdom of heaven" imply that little ones already belong to God's family.

It does not follow that all who are baptized as infants will grow up to be faithful Christians. God has done his part, but the parents and the church must do theirs. The parents have a direct responsibility in bringing up the child, by their example and their teaching, in the "nurture and admonition of the Lord." That ceases only when the baptized child confirms his baptismal vow by joining the church and receiving his first Lord's Supper. The church, too, through the teaching of the Sunday school and the interest and care of its members shares in the responsibility for the Christian upbringing of the child. There is also a responsibility resting on the child himself. The child is held responsible for the right use of the privileges he has received. To refuse to become a full member of Christ's church, would be to insult the God who has protected the child, and the fellowship of Christians which has educated him in Christian ways.

2. The Lord's Supper

There are differences in the administration of the Lord's Supper among Protestant churches, but its meaning is the same for all Protestants. Anglicans and Methodists come forward to the altar or holy table to receive the elements, kneeling. Baptists, Congregationalists, and Presbyterians receive the bread and wine in the sitting posture, as those who are guests at Christ's table. Anglicans take Communion usually once a week, Baptists and Congregationalists usually once a fortnight, and Presbyterians in England bimonthly and in Scotland usually once a quarter.

The meaning and authority of the Lord's Supper or Holy Communion is, however, the same for all. The New

Testament authority for the Lord's Supper is found in I
Cor. 11:23-26 (see also Matt. 26:26-30; Mark 14:23-26; and
Luke 22:14-20). Jesus instituted this sacrament in Jerusalem the night before his crucifixion. He intended it to
be a memorial to him that would bring the disciples comfort in their loneliness, and strength in their weakness
when he should have left them. The mere repetition of the
acts of breaking the bread and pouring out the wine would
bring back to their remembrance not only his voice but his
presence, and they would remember the new covenant
which had been won for mankind by his broken body and
shed blood. Wherever this sacrament has been celebrated
it has made real to Christian disciples the spiritual presence
of their Lord. In the catacombs of Rome, or in modern
concentration camps; in stately cathedral, or in quiet
village chapel; the Lord's Supper has been the meeting
place of Christ and his followers.

What, then, is the meaning of the Lord's Supper? First,
it is a memorial. "This do," said our Lord, "in remembrance of me." It is in particular a commemoration of the
death of Christ. The sacrament declares the message of the
Cross. We understand anew what it cost God to forgive
sin, and how sin is rebellion against God. We also understand the depth of the love of God, who "so loved the
world, that he gave his only begotten Son, that whosoever
believeth on him should not perish, but have eternal life."

Second, the Communion is not a tribute to a dead
Leader, but a tryst with a living Lord. As its name implies,
it is a real communion between Christ and us. He fulfills
his promise, "Lo, I am with you alway, even unto the
end of the world." Through our obedience and faith in
celebrating this memorial, he comes to our souls, bringing
forgiveness, renewing our desire to serve him, teaching us

what his will is, giving us new strength to serve him, healing the sorrows and disappointments of our life, and reconciling us to our heavenly Father.

Third, the Lord's Supper also has a future reference. "But I say unto you, I will not drink henceforth of this fruit of the vine, until that day when I drink it new with you in my Father's kingdom" (Matt. 26:29). The Lord's Supper points forward to that day when his disciples shall share with him the joy and glory of eternal life.

Fourth, the Lord's Supper is a pledge of our loyalty to Christ and to one another. The *sacramentum* was the oath of allegiance to his emperor taken by a Roman soldier. This sacrament is also our promise of fealty to the Lord. And, as he is the Vine and we are the branches, so are we knitted together in the unity of his body the Church.

III

WORSHIP AND LIFE

CHAPTER 14

Why Go to Church?

THE QUESTIONER IS UNCONSCIOUSLY IN THE POSITION OF THE
Devil's dupe, described by C. S. Lewis. He is thinking of
the Church, not as the community of Christians that transcends centuries and traverses continents, but as a building
in which religious persons meet for religious exercises:

All your patient sees is the half-finished, sham Gothic erec-
tion on the new building estate. When he goes inside, he sees
the local grocer with rather an oily expression on his face
bustling up to offer him one shiny little book containing a
liturgy which neither of them understands, and one shabby
little book containing corrupt texts of a number of religious
lyrics, mostly bad, and in very small print. When he gets to
his pew and looks round him he sees just that selection of his
neighbours whom he has hitherto avoided.[1]

More than that, the visitor to the church may find there
the disreputable and the hypocritical, and he will certainly
find sinners. The Church is not yet without "spot or
wrinkle or any such thing." This is its "wretchedness," as
its "greatness" is that "Christ . . . loved the church, and
gave himself up for it." Both its wretchedness and its greatness constitute claims on the individual. The supreme

[1] *The Screwtape Letters* (New York: The Macmillan Co., 1947), pp.
15-16.

authority of the Church is that it has pleased God to extend the work of the incarnate Lord through his church. It was brought into being as the new "Chosen People," the new Israel, by the mighty acts of God in the incarnation, the cross, the resurrection, and the ascension of our Lord, and in the descent of the Holy Spirit at Pentecost. That is its divine origin and charter. It has also pleased God to renew and maintain its life through the centuries as a saved and saving community.

It would not have occurred to God's faithful people under the old or new dispensations to question the necessity for churchgoing. The psalmist, for instance, who has a deep personal communion with God, does not regard this as a substitute for corporate worship. On the contrary, he declares:

> I will pay my vows unto the Lord,
> Yea, in the presence of all his people.

Our Lord himself attended divine worship in temple and synagogue, and "the servant is not above his Lord," that he should be able to dispense with the means of grace. The apostolic Church came of age "when the day of Pentecost was now come" and "they were all together in one place." Its activities were all corporate activities: "And they continued steadfastly in the apostles' teaching and fellowship, in the breaking of bread and the prayers."

In the light of the biblical evidence, our Lord's example and commands, and in the experience of the Church, the definition of Whitehead, that "religion is what a man does with his solitariness," is seen to be one-sided. Much more balanced is the judgment of Berdyaev:

It does not follow that religion is but an individual event

104

and the privilege of a certain number of isolated souls. On the contrary, religion not only binds and unites man to God, but it is the essential bond between man and his fellow-beings; it is both community and communion.[2]

The personal and social sides of man's nature receive their full meaning in the community of Christ.

Already the answer to this question has shaped itself. I should go to church to share in the life of the Body of Christ, the redeemed and redeeming community.

The question may now be narrowed to consider, "Why should I attend worship?" Four reasons are compelling, in their united impetus:

1. The first purpose of Christian worship is thanksgiving. It is the glad response of Christians to the holy, redemptive love of God made known in Jesus Christ. "We love, because he first loved us." "One great experience," says Heiler, "dominates the primitive Church: the assurance of salvation bestowed in Christ and the yearning for the speedy fulfilment of the Kingdom of God." [3] This is the perennial theme of Christian worship that sounds through the liturgies of Christendom, in prayers and in hymns and psalms. In days of persecution the song of the redeemed in heaven breaks through the menacing clouds, as it did in the days of the author of Revelation, to cheer the struggling saints. In days of the stability and recognition of the Church, still the worshiping congregation united with the Church triumphant:

The glorious company of the apostles praise Thee,
The goodly fellowship of the prophets praise Thee,

[2] Nicholas Berdyaev, *Solitude and Society,* tr. George Reavey (New York: Charles Scribner's Sons, 1938).

[3] Friedrich Heiler, *Prayer,* tr. and ed. Samuel McComb (New York: Oxford University Press, 1932).

The noble army of martyrs praise Thee,
The holy Church throughout the world doth acknowledge
Thee.

The congregation, says Ignatius, "will sing praise to Him
as a great choir." It will rehearse the mighty acts of God
in Christ culminating in the founding of the Church and
the renewing of her life. Worship is, therefore, the glad
acknowledgment of God's love in Christ.

2. If worship is primarily an offering, it is necessarily
the offering of the Church, not the offering of a collection
of individuals. It is the worship of Christ's own church, his
body, of which he is the head. "We, who are many, are one
body in Christ." So Christian worship must be common
worship.

There is, of course, a place for private prayer—that is
the inner chamber. But that is no substitute for "common
prayer." Indeed, to practice the presence of God only in
private, is spiritually dangerous to the individual soul.
The individual who tries to live apart from the beloved
community, and despises its ordinances and means of grace,
is a prey to pride. His life is like that of the Lowells,
caricatured by Samuel Bushnell:

> I come from good old Boston,
> The home of the bean and the cod;
> Where the Cabots speak only to Lowells,
> And the Lowells speak only to God!

The Christian is not called to serve God alone on a desert
island, like Robinson Crusoe. Indeed, if he has an "island
complex," he is robbing himself of citizenship in a mighty
commonwealth, for he should come "unto mount Zion,
and unto the city of the living God, the heavenly Jerusa-

lem, and to innumerable hosts of angels, to the general assembly and church of the firstborn who are enrolled in heaven" (Heb. 12:22-23a).

His sin is greater, for he is dismembering the Body of Christ. No servant of our Lord has the right to say to another: "I have no need of you." It is impossible sociologically; it is more foolish to attempt to say it of the Church. It is as irresponsible as "if the foot shall say, Because I am not the hand, I am not of the body; it is not therefore not of the body." The Christian life is incomplete for the individual, as it is for the Body of Christ, by a refusal to participate in its worship and life.

3. The third purpose of Christian worship is "edification." By attendance at the worship of the church the Christian is built up in the faith and love and hope of the Christian life. This is his time of discipleship. He is being built into the Body of Christ, through the ordinances.

The Church's liturgy is thus her reading of the Scriptures in which Jesus Christ her life is declared, and her preaching from the Scriptures in which she tries to listen to His voice speaking directly to her condition, and her celebration of the Sacraments in which she acknowledges that she holds her life from Jesus Christ and is constantly forgiven, renewed, and maintained in faith by His grace, and her Church Meeting, where as representatives of the New Humanity her members meet to order their life together according to the will of Jesus Christ who has given Himself to them in Word and Sacrament.[4]

A secondary meaning of "edification" is that the members of the Body shall learn the art of prayer by assembling

[4] Daniel T. Jenkins, *Prayer and the Service of God* (New York: Morehouse-Gorham Co., Inc., 1945). Used by permission of Morehouse-Gorham Co., Inc., and Faber & Faber, Ltd.

together. The humble beginner learns the maturity of the saints in common prayer.

The prayer of the congregation is meant to lift the individual to a higher stage of devotion. Narrow self-seeking wishes should be silenced in the presence of the congregation. The little and weak who come to the meeting with low and earthly thoughts, should be carried to heights of religious yearning, should pray as the strong and creative pray: those who do not know what true prayer is, should here learn to pray and practice the art.[5]

A further meaning of "edification" is that here the Christian should learn to forgive others, having himself been forgiven by God in Christ. By the transforming power of the Holy Spirit, that will become possible. By the intercessory prayers he will be enabled to view the world through the compassionate and holy eyes of Christ, and to enter into the perpetual passion of the Saviour, interceding for his world. He will know the meaning of Luther's experience that "to praise the Lord with gladness is not a work of man; it is rather a joyful suffering, and the work of God alone." [6]

In all these manifold ways is the Christian built up, edified, in the Body of Christ.

4. The worship of the Church is the stimulus to the Christian life in the world. The service of God ("liturgy") leads inevitably to the service of men for God's sake. Indeed, this is worship in its widest sense, the offering of man's life in the Church and in the world to the glory of God. This is the meaning of the fine opening to the West-

[5] Heiler, *Prayer*.
[6] *A Compend of Luther's Theology*, ed. Hugh Thomson Kerr, Jr. (Philadelphia: Westminster Press, 1943).

minster Shorter Catechism: "Man's chief end is to glorify God and to enjoy him forever." The same conviction was finely expressed by that stalwart Puritan, Lucy Hutchinson, thus:

> By Christianity I intend that universal habit of grace which is wrought in a soul by the regenerating Spirit of God, whereby the whole creature is resigned up into the Divine will and love, and all its actions designed to the obedience and glory of its Maker.[7]

Worship is, therefore, an incentive to Christian citizenship, to Christian labor, to Christian witness, that "the kingdom of the world [may] become the kingdom of our Lord, and of his Christ."

In short, we should go to church to praise God, to share in the common life of Christ's body, to be built up in Christian faith and love, and to share in the witness and service of the Church to the world.

---

[7] *Memoirs of the Life of Colonel Hutchinson* (New York: E. P. Dutton & Co., 1906).

CHAPTER 15

Why a Place of Worship?

THIS QUESTION IS PUT BY TWO SETS OF PEOPLE. ONE GROUP, described by William Temple, former Archbishop of Canterbury, as "blue-domers" [1] are in reality declaring that they find it more helpful to worship God in nature, "under the blue dome of heaven." Another group insists that a church edifice, with its formal atmosphere and ecclesiastical furniture, is out of keeping with the simple and informal house-meetings of the first-century Church.

The attraction of worshiping God "in the cathedral of pines, in the diocese of Nature" is not to be denied. Emile Cammaerts puts the case as strongly as possible, recollecting his youthful romanticism:

> I never missed a Sunday walk and thought that I found in a wood a stronger inspiration than that which I could find in a church. The music of birds and waving branches was better than any organ, and the smell of dead leaves and pines scorched by the earth better than incense. The trunks of beeches and the high vaults of their branches were the columns and arches of my cathedral. [2]

But the same author, on mature consideration, declares that his earlier attachment to nature-worship was sentimental and misanthropic in character. The same charges might justly be made against many nature worshipers.

The charge of sentimentalism cannot be substantiated

[1] *How Christians Worship*, ed. J. Eric Fenn (London: Student Christian Movement Press, 1942), p. 20.

[2] *Flower of Grass* (New York: Harper & Bros., 1945).

in the best nature poetry, as, for instance, that of William Wordsworth. But even he, according to Aldous Huxley, would not have been a nature mystic if he had lived in the tropics, instead of in the Lake district. Sentimentalizing over nature is seen typically in a poem of Dorothy Frances Gurney, who writes:

> The kiss of the sun for pardon,
> The song of the birds for mirth,—
> One is nearer God's heart in a garden
> Than anywhere else on earth.[3]

The Christian may find in the loveliness of the rose a hint of the divine Artist; but for the revelation of God's heart he would go not to an English garden, but to the garden of Gethsemane, and for pardon to the cross.

Paul Elmer More, the American humanist, provides an astringent for nature mysticism in his meditation on Symond's Yat. Beneath him were birds sailing on seas of air, and gentle oxen grazing placidly on the riverside meadows:

To the eye it was a widespread theatre of joy and a masque of peaceful beauty. Until I thought of what lay beneath the surface. Here in fact was an army of countless individuals, each driven on by an instinctive lust for life as if engaged on a vast internecine warfare—each blade of grass fighting for its place in the sun, and obtaining it by the suppression of some other plant, each animal preying for sustenance upon some other form of life. It is a system of ruthless competition and remorseless extermination.

His final verdict on the scene is: "From every spot of the

[3] From "The Lord God Planted a Garden." Used by permission of Burns, Oates, and Washbourne, Ltd.

earth rises continually the battle-cry of Nature: *Væ victis*" [meaning, "Woe to the conquered"].

The nature worshipers may be reminded that it is easy to worship God when the golden corn dances in the summer sunlight; but it is more difficult to sing, "Praise ye the Lord," as a snake glides through the grass toward a hypnotized bird. The viper, the hawk, the bacillus, are equally parts of nature with the primrose and the deer. The fact is that we can be sure of God's overruling beneficence in nature, only after we have seen his lovingkindness in grace. We can thank him for our creation, only after we have seen his re-creation of man through Christ our Lord.

The second charge against "open-air worship" is that it conduces to misanthropy, or is the result of such dislike of mankind. The previous chapter tried to explain that Christian worship is essentially the worship of the redeemed community, not the voluntary association of like-minded persons. Clearly, nature worship is, by contrast, a refusal to worship God in the way that he has ordained: "in the presence of all his people."

This is not, of course, to deny that occasionally Christian worship out-of-doors may be permitted. This has been the custom of the churches when, for instance, the people have not come to the house of God, and the Church has had to go to the people. Franciscan friars and Methodist field preachers conducted memorable services among the uncommitted. Similarly, in days of persecution Christians, of necessity, worshiped God wherever they could meet in comparative safety. In the third century the faithful worshiped in the catacombs of Rome; in the sixteenth and seventeenth centuries the Nonconformists worshiped in the fields or barns of England. But special circumstances demanded emergency measures. The most convenient and regular place for Christian worship is the church or chapel.

Finally, it is not suggested that due appreciation of the works of God the creator should be excluded from Christian worship. The Scriptures encourage this. Genesis, the Psalms, Job—to mention only a few books of the Bible—as well as the teaching of our Lord, bid us "praise [God] for his . . . wonderful works to the children of men" and to "consider the lilies of the field." The Apostles' Creed begins: "I believe in God, the Father Almighty, Maker of heaven and earth."

The General Thanksgiving preserves the true balance in its comprehensive catalogue of gratitude:

We bless thee for our creation, preservation, and all the blessings of this life; but, *above all*, for thine inestimable love in the redemption of the world by our Lord Jesus Christ; for the means of grace, and for the hope of glory.

The Christian family fittingly adores God in God's house as God's household of faith.

It remains to answer those who aver that formal worship in a church is a departure from the simplicity and spontaneity of the house fellowships of the church of the apostles. This criticism was finely answered by Richard Hooker in the following words:

The Church of Christ which was in Jerusalem, and held that profession which had not the public allowance and countenance of authority, could not so long use the exercise of Christian religion, but in private only. So that as Jews they had access to the Temple and synagogues, where God was served after the custom of the Law; but that for which they did as Christians, they were of necessity forced otherwhere to assemble themselves.[4]

The Christians met in houses for their distinctively Christian exercises, because they could not celebrate the Lord's Supper in synagogue or temple. What was an irksome necessity for them, ought not to be elevated into an example for future generations freed from the restrictions imposed on the early Christians.

While it is true that worship is acceptable to God wherever it is offered, so long as it be "in spirit and in truth," yet

the very majesty and holiness of the place where God is worshipped, hath *in regard of us* great virtue, force, and efficacy, for that it serveth as a sensible help to stir up devotion, and in that respect no doubt bettereth even our holiest and best actions in this kind.[5]

Thus the building in which the Church meets for worship is more than a convenient roof and walls; it is, or ought to be, a "help to stir up devotion." This is achieved by its associations and its symbols.

Ancient cathedrals or historic parish churches remind the worshipers that "others have laboured, and ye are entered into their labour"; that the Christian church has weathered many storms and that "the gates of Hades shall not prevail against it." Furthermore, they serve as a perpetual reminder of the communion of saints. A Puritan meetinghouse of the seventeenth century is also capable of suggesting the same reflections.

The chief advantage of a Christian edifice is that it

[4] *Of the Laws of Ecclesiastical Polity* V. II. 2. (Cf. Acts 1:13; 2:1, 46.)
[5] *Ibid.* V. 16. 2.

preaches to the eye, as the sermons preach to the ear. The central cross on rood screen or on communion table declares the costliness of our redemption. The stained-glass windows portray, it may be, the prophets, apostles, and martyrs, and remind the worshipers of the "great cloud of witnesses." Or they may illustrate some incident in the life of our Lord: his holy nativity, his temptations in the wilderness, his miracles, his crucifixion, his resurrection, or the final judgment at which he is to be the arbiter of human destiny. This is all visual teaching of the Christian faith.

The font itself is a reminder that the promises of the gospel belong by right to the children of Christian parents. The altar or communion table declares the centrality of the sacrament, and the pulpit or lectern, on which rests the Bible, is a potent reminder to "search the scriptures," for they contain "the word of life."

The very beauty of the building is an incentive to "worship the Lord in the beauty of holiness." Even the Puritan Milton could write:

> But let my due feet never fail,
> To walk the studious Cloysters pale.
> And love the high embowe'd Roof,
> With antick Pillars massy proof,
> And storied Windows richly dight,
> Casting a dimm religious light.[6]

In conclusion, the Christian communities have ordinarily worshiped in cathedrals, churches, chapels, or meetinghouses, because corporate worship demanded a convenient edifice. In the second place, they have found that the associations and the symbols have assisted the wor-

6 "Il Penseroso."

shipers in their devotions. This chapter concludes by asking
the questioner:

Can we judge it a thing seemly for any man to go about the
building of a house to the God of heaven with no other appearance, than if his end were to rear up a kitchen or a parlour
for his own use? [7]

[7] Hooker op. cit. V. 12. 1.

CHAPTER 16

Why So Many Kinds of Worship?

THE BEWILDERING VARIETY OF FORMS OF CHRISTIAN WORSHIP calls for explanation. No brief answer can be given, but any attempt to provide an explanation must allow for three factors: (1) *historical*—to account for the rise of the different forms of worship; (2) *psychological*—since the varieties of Christian worship are partly due to temperamental and national approaches to worship; (3) *ecumenical*—because there is an underlying unity beneath the multiformity of Christian worship.

1. The historical factors have already been considered in the earlier chapters of this book. Here a few observations will be in order, instead of attempting a conspectus of the causes for variety. The historic basis of the Christian revelation would ensure a fundamental unity in the structure of Christian worship from the days of the apostles. From the beginning this structure appears to have been twofold: a synagogue type of service and a eucharist or upper-room service, for the celebration of the Lord's Supper. Within that framework there must have been considerable latitude, since the choice of psalms and hymns would vary and the earliest prayers were probably extemporary in kind. By the fourth century A.D. the "liturgy" (used in this context as a set order of service) took the place of the earlier fluid rites. But even then different Christian centers had developed their own liturgies. The three most famous "families" of liturgy were the Roman, the Egyptian, and the Syrian, not to mention the liturgies of St. Basil (Asia Minor) and St. Mark (Alexandria) which contain early

material, but are heavily overlaid by fifth- and sixth-century additions.[1]

Thus the early variety within the framework was perpetuated by the different local traditions of the Christian communities. The eleventh-century division between the Eastern and Western churches tended to perpetuate the differences between the two main branches of Christendom, henceforward to go their separate ways. During the medieval period further developments in Christian worship ensued as the experience of the churches was enriched by the addition of new devotional materials. Finally, the Reformation with its insistence on a return to a worship more biblical in basis, and resulting in the formation of the different denominations of the Protestant churches, added to the complex variety of Christian worship, varying from the "pruned Catholicism" of the Lutheran churches to the almost complete absence of ceremonial in the worship of the Society of Friends. The greater part of the variety is thus due to historical and geographical factors.

2. It is sometimes maintained that the differences in worship are due to differences in national and individual temperament. Thus it is sometimes said that the difference between the worship of the Anglican Church and that of the Free Churches is that the former prefer their worship "tuppeny colored," while the latter incline to "penny plain." While members of both communions may claim that they exert a conscious temperamental preference, this cannot be said of their founders. The progenitors of the Free Churches, the Puritans, did not object to ceremonial on grounds of temperament. On the contrary, they claimed

[1] The reader is referred to J. H. Srawley's *The Early History of the Liturgy*, or to ch. viii of Dom Gregory Dix's *The Shape of the Liturgy*, for both evidence and explanation.

that the New Testament offered no support for much of the ceremonial of the Established Church. For their part the Anglicans claimed that their worship had the sanction of hallowed usage, and the authority of the primitive Church. Personal preference or æsthetic considerations played no part in the decisions of either group. In present days, their successors may claim that they are "high" or "low" by choice; but often they are merely asserting that they understand the traditions in which they were reared and prefer them to the other alternatives. In that limited sense alone does temperament affect the continued divergence of liturgical traditions.

It may also be claimed that to some degree national characteristics account for the variations in the historic liturgies. But this, like all generalizations, is subject to exceptions and modifications. Dom Gregory Dix, while stressing that the unity of the liturgies is more remarkable than their diversities, insists that because liturgies express the life of Christian peoples, therefore their natural characteristics "do to a large extent enter into their religious life to be supernaturalised by grace." He offers this interesting summary of the national characteristics expressed in the historic liturgies of Christendom:

The perfervid devotionalism of the Syrian, . . . the ceremoniousness of the Byzantine, with his love of etiquette—the *naïveté* of the Copt and his love of repetitions—the French mutability and love of some new thing—that special "tenderness" of English devotion, which manifests itself in a love of rather setimental hymns and vocal prayers in the first Anglo-Saxon private prayer books that we have—the prosaic practicality and the almost stuffy conservatism of the local church of Rome—these things do not change from century to century.[2]

[2] *The Shape of the Liturgy*, p. 432.

While these national differences of temperament color the ceremonial and the phrasing of the prayers, the unity of the structure of Christian worship remains.

3. Thus the question is answered: "Christian worship in its multiformity is essentially a series of variations on a single theme." The ecumenical movement,[3] whose motto is, "That they all may be one," has, by its conferences, enabled Christians of widely differing traditions to understand their fundamental Christian unity in faith, worship, and witness. All Christian worship is basically our offering of obedience and gratitude to God's giving in Christ our Lord, foretold in the Old Testament, fulfilled in the New Testament, remembered and received anew in divine worship, in sermon and sacraments. That response to the gospel of God is given by the Body of Christ in prayer and praise and dedication. In stately cathedral or in hillside chapel, in parish church or in meetinghouse, in whatever tongue, whether with ceremonial or with only the barest minimum, in set liturgy or in freer forms of worship (or in silence, occasionally broken by the devout meditations of the obedient servants of Christ, as in the case of the Society of Friends), it is the mighty acts of God in the redemption of the world through our Lord Jesus Christ that are re-presented, and the benefits of which are appropriated. Uniformity in approach there is not; but unity in obedience and in adoring gratitude transcends all differences. "For ye all are one . . . in Christ Jesus." (Gal. 3:28.)

---

[3] *Ecumenical*—meaning "universal." In this context applied to the movement aiming at the union of the Christian churches.

CHAPTER 17

My Part in Worship

WORSHIP, AS WE HAVE SEEN, IS THE RESPONSE OF THE BODY of Christians to the revelation of God in Jesus Christ. The part of the worshiper is therefore to co-operate in this response. In the usual and regular services of the churches, three responsive actions are allowed for this co-operation: the "Amens" in prayer; the praise in hymns and chants; and the offertory.

Churches which use a liturgy give the worshiper a larger part in the prayers. Anglicans, for instance, recite the General Thanksgiving and the General Confession together. They also in the Litany, and elsewhere, make their response in the suffrages, and in the Preface to the Prayer of Consecration in the Order for Holy Communion. The Free Churches often confine the response to the prayers to the single important word *Amen*. This is not intended to be a mere mark of punctuation, a liturgical full stop, as, for instance, the end of a Shakespearian scene is indicated by a concluding couplet. It is intended to be the conscious sign of the congregation's entering into the prayers of the minister and of their approval.

The second responsive action of the congregation is the singing of praise. The hymnbook is so arranged as to provide suitable thanksgivings for each season of the Christian year—from Advent, through Christmas, Epiphany, Lent, Passiontide, Eastertide, Ascensiontide, Whitsuntide, to Trinity Sunday. At each season there is a direct response to the part of God's revelation in Christ commemorated at that time. Other hymns celebrate the natural seasons

121

and times: morning and evening, spring, summer, harvest, autumn, winter. Another group of hymns, more general in character, celebrates the benefits of the Christian life, the means of grace and hope of glory. The Christian is thus equipped by the hymnbook he uses (containing the devotions of many centuries and many traditions) to "rejoice in the Lord always."

The third responsive action is the offertory. The monetary collection of the present day corresponds to the gifts in kind which were brought by the members of the primitive Church. These were voluntary offerings, not taxes, made out of a glad recognition of what the Christian faith had done for them. They were, in fact, the material symbols of thankful hearts. They constituted a real witness to the Christian faith. The same should be true of the present-day worshiper's contribution to the offertory. The attitude to be cultivated is indicated by Oswald Milligan, as follows:

The New Testament bears witness that such gifts are acceptable to Him who sits over against the treasury not in accordance with their amount, but rather in the proportion they bear to the giver's means, for only thus do they typify a spiritual action. It is this note, that the offering we give represents the value we set out to express, which we wish to recover and emphasize in our services to-day.[1]

It is not to be inferred that the part of the worshiper is exhausted by these three responsive actions in Christian worship. These three actions are expressions made by the voice or the hand. But equally important is the response of silent obedience made by the worshiper during the reading of the Scriptures and the preaching of the sermon. "He that hath ears, let him hear," said our Lord. The

[1] *The Ministry of Worship* (New York: Oxford University Press, 1941).

reverent attention given to the declaration of the revelation of God is also co-operation in the worship. Indeed, inattention during lessons and sermon is destructive of the true spirit of worship. This was finely expressed by W. L. Watkinson, when visiting a country church. When he was about to give out the text for the sermon, the lights were lowered. "Put up the lights," said he, "I can't see my notes." Then, when the lights were turned up again, he said to the congregation, "You are my notes." Minister and people, the one by speaking and the rest by listening, co-operate in the lessons and the sermon.

There are also other ways in which to participate in worship. To begin with, the very presence of the worshiper is an act of worship, a token of his dependence upon God and of his membership of the family of Christ. It has also an inspirational value for others, as encouragement. The contribution made to worship is not lessened because the worshiper has come, on a particular occasion, from a sense of duty, rather than out of delight. True, on such occasions, the worshiper is likely to "get less out of" the service, but he gives more in the recognition that the attendance at worship is an act of obedience, not a response to a mood or a whim.

Moreover, in the silence before a service begins, the worshiper is able to prepare for the worship. In this act of recollection, of petition, or of intercession (or all three), the individual is contributing to the reality of the worship. In a larger sense, the living of the Christian life in the preceding week is also a preparation for worship, both by edification in the Christian faith through prayer and Bible reading, and by service in the name of Christ. In all these ways by preparation and participation the individual takes his part in worship.

Finally, there is an intimate relation between worship and life, between our devotions in church and our service in the world.

Service can be no substitute for worship. Indeed, as Kenneth Kirk, former Bishop of Oxford, has reminded us, service without worship becomes "the service of patronage":

Yet apart from an atmosphere of worship, every act of service avails only to inflate the agent's sense of patronage. He is the doctor, humanity is his patient: he is the Samaritan, his neighbour the crippled wayfarer: he is the instructor, others are merely his pupils. Gratitude (if they show gratitude) only confirms his conviction of his own importance; resentment (if they resent his services) only ministers to the glow of self-esteem with which he comforts himself in secret.[2]

By contrast, "the glory of worship is to elicit the grace of humility." Our worship has at its center a cross, the divine token of disinterested service on the part of One who "humbled himself, becoming obedient even unto death, yea, the death of the cross."

If service can be no substitute for worship, equally worship must issue in service. Indeed, if our worship is genuine, we are driven by it to holy and sacrificial service of our brethren for whom Christ died. In a succinct definition of the purpose of worship, the Second World Conference on Faith and Order declared in 1937: "The function of the Church is to glorify God in adoration and sacrificial service."[3]

Love to God must beget love to our brethren.

[2] *The Vision of God* (abr. ed.; New York: Longmans, Green & Co., 1934).
[3] *The Second World Conference on Faith and Order,* ed. Leonard Hodgson (New York: The Macmillan Co., 1938).

Furthermore, in the widest sense, worship is the glorifying of God in common life. Unless both conversation and conduct witness to the standards of Christ, worship is mere escapism: it has ceased to be inspirational and redemptive. Devotion to Christ demands ethical proofs in daily life. "I am the vine, ye are the branches." The seal of this relationship is that "he that abideth in me, and I in him, the same beareth much fruit" (John 15:5). Worship is, therefore, a life dedicated to God, not a fugitive hour in a week devoted to unscrupulous business. It is a life lived out in the presence of God, for his glory and the benefit of mankind. To that end, the Christian prays, with George Herbert:

> Teach me, my God and King,
> In all things Thee to see,
> And what I do in anything,
> To do it as for Thee.

BIBLIOGRAPHY

TEXTS AND COMMENTARIES

Eastern Liturgy

Brightman, Frank E. (ed.). *Liturgies, Eastern and Western.* New York: Oxford University Press, 1896. Vol. I.

Neale, J. M., and Littledale, R. F. *Translations of the Primitive Liturgies* (Eastern). 2nd ed. London, 1869.

Pre-Reformation and Roman Liturgy

Missale Romanum. Editio II juxta typicam Vaticanam amplificata I. New York, 1942.

Parsch, Pius. *The Liturgy of the Mass.* Translated by Frederic C. Eckhoff. 6th ed. St. Louis: B. Herder Book Co., 1941.

Rituale Romanum. Desclee ed. Romae, Typis Soc. S. Joannis Evangelistae, 1914.

West, R. C. (ed.). *Western Liturgies.* New York: The Macmillan Co., 1938.

Lutheran Liturgy

Common Service Book of the Lutheran Church. Philadelphia: Board of Publication of the United Lutheran Church in America, 1930 and later imprints.

Reed, Luther D. *The Lutheran Liturgy: A Study of the Common Service of the Lutheran Church in America.* Philadelphia: Muhlenberg Press, 1947.

Anglican and Episcopalian Liturgy

The Book of Common Prayer, with the additions and deviations proposed in 1928. New York: Oxford University Press, 1928.

The Book of Common Prayer and Administration of the Sacraments and Other Rites and Ceremonies of the Church, According to the Use of the Protestant Episcopal Church in the United States of America. New York: Oxford University Press, 1938 and later printings.

Shepherd, Massey H. *The Oxford American Prayer Book Commentary.* New York: Oxford University Press, 1950.

Presbyterian Worship

The Book of Common Order of the Church of Scotland. New York: Oxford University Press, 1940.

The Book of Common Worship. Philadelphia: Publication Division of the Board of Christian Education of the Presbyterian Church in the U.S.A., 1946.

Methodist Worship

The Book of Offices (Methodist Church of Great Britain). London, 1936.

The Book of Worship for Church and Home (Methodist Church of the United States). New York and Nashville: The Methodist Publishing House, 1944 and later imprints.

Harmon, Nolan B. *The Rites and Rituals of Episcopal Methodism.* Nashville: Publishing House of the Methodist Episcopal Church, South, 1926.

_____. *Understanding The Methodist Church.* New York and Nashville: Abingdon Press, 1955.

Congregational Worship

The Book of Congregational Worship. London, 1920.

A Book of Public Worship: For the Use of Congregationalists. Compiled by W. J. F. Huxtable *et al.* New York: Oxford University Press, 1948.

A Book of Worship for Free Churches. Prepared under the direction of the General Council of the Congregational Christian Churches in the United States. New York: Oxford University Press, 1948.

A Manual for Ministers. London: Independent Press, 1936.

Baptist Worship

Aubrey, M. E. (ed.). *A Minister's Manual.* London: Kingsgate Press, n.d.

Patterson, David Tait (ed.). *The Call to Worship.* London: Carey Press, 1938.

Quaker Worship

Brinton, Howard H. *Friends for 300 Years.* New York: Harper & Bros., 1952. Ch. IV.

Hodgkin, L. Violet. *Silent Worship: The Way of Wonder* (Swarthmore lecture). London, 1919.

GENERAL AND HISTORICAL STUDIES

Bishop, Edmund. *Liturgica Historica.* New York: Oxford University Press, 1918.

Davies, Horton. *The Worship of the English Puritans.* Westminster, Eng.: The Dacre Press, 1948.

Dix, Gregory. *The Shape of the Liturgy.* London: A. & C. Black, 1945.

Duchesne, Louis. *Christian Worship: Its Origin and Evolution.*

Translated by M. L. McClure. 5th ed. New York: The Macmillan Co., 1931.

Fortescue, Adrian. *The Mass: A Study of the Roman Liturgy*. New York: Longmans, Green & Co., 1917.

Heiler, Friedrich. *The Spirit of Worship*. Translated by W. Montgomery. New York: George H. Doran Co., 1926.

Hislop, David H. *Our Heritage in Public Worship*. New York: Charles Scribner's Sons, 1935.

Jones, Ilion T. *A Historical Approach to Evangelical Worship*. New York and Nashville: Abingdon Press, 1954.

Macdonald, Alexander B. *Christian Worship in the Primitive Church*. New York: Charles Scribner's Sons, 1934.

Maxwell, William D. *An Outline of Christian Worship*. New York: Oxford University Press, 1936 and later editions.

Meland, Bernard E. *Modern Man's Worship: A Search for Reality in Religion*. New York: Harper & Bros., 1934.

Micklem, Edward R. *Our Approach to God: A Study in Public Worship*. London: Hodder & Stoughton, 1934.

Micklem, Nathaniel. *Christian Worship: Studies in Its History and Meaning*. New York: Oxford University Press, 1936.

Morison, Stanley. *English Prayer Books*. (*Problems of Worship*, eds. W. R. Matthews and F. W. Dwelly, Vol. I.) New York: The Macmillan Co., 1944.

Otto, Rudolf. *The Idea of the Holy*. Translated by John W. Harvey. Rev. ed. New York: Oxford University Press, 1925.

Ratcliff, E. C. "Christian Worship and Liturgy," *The Study of Theology*, ed. Kenneth E. Kirk. New York: Harper & Bros., 1939.

Short, Ernest H. *A History of Religious Architecture*. Rev. ed. New York: The Macmillan Co., 1936.

Sperry, Willard L. *Reality in Worship*. New York: The Macmillan Co., 1925.

Srawley, J. H. *The Early History of the Liturgy*. New York: The Macmillan Co., 1913 and 1956 rev. ed.

Underhill, Evelyn. *Worship*. New York: Harper & Bros., 1937.

Vogt, Von Ogden. *Art and Religion*. New Haven: Yale University Press, 1921.

Ways of Worship. The Report of a Theological Commission of the World Council of Churches. Eds. Pehr Edwall *et al*. New York: Harper & Bros., 1951.

Will, Robert. *Le Culte: Etude d'Histoire et de Philosophie Religieuses*. 3 vols. Paris, 1925-35.